To Inclusion and Beyond

Evangelical and affirming LGBTQ+ relationships and equal marriage

Danny Brierley

STATEN HOUSE

Staten House

About the Author

Danny Brierley is Minister of Chester Road Baptist Church, having previously served churches in Stourbridge and Altrincham, UK. He has an unusual mix of church ministry, Christian charity (Head of Youth Services, Oasis UK), commercial (Executive Search 'head hunter') and education (RE teaching) experience, with a 'red thread' of encouraging people to explore issues of faith, identity, and purpose. After a 20+ year writing gap, he can no longer be considered prolific.

Other books by Danny
- **Joined Up: an introduction to youth work and ministry** (Authentic/ Spring Harvest, 2003)

- **What Every Volunteer Youth Worker Should Know** (Authentic/ Spring Harvest, 2003)

- **Growing Community: making groups work with young people** (Authentic/ Spring Harvest, 2003)

- **Young People and Small Groups** (Scripture Union, 1997)

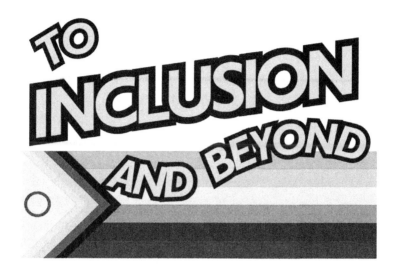

TO INCLUSION AND BEYOND

Evangelical and affirming
LGBTQ+ relationships
and equal marriage

First published in Great Britain in 2024

British Library Cataloguing-in-Publication Data

In accordance with the Legal Deposit Libraries Act 2003, a catalogue record for this book is available from the British Library, as well as the Bodleian Library (Oxford University), Cambridge University Library, the National Library of Scotland, the National Library of Wales, and the Library of Trinity College, Dublin.

ISBN:

Paperback: 979-8-88940-619-8

Hardcover: 979-8-88940-819-2

eBook: 979-8-88940-616-7

First printed in Great Britain.

Contents

Preface

I wrote this book by accident. I didn't mean to, it just happened. For many years my Evangelical church tradition told me 'homosexuality' was a sin. I just accepted it as 'gospel'. For all our talk of grace and mercy, we seemed more familiar with condemnation, guilt, and shame. Yet, as I experienced God and studied the Bible, I began to feel uneasy: God appeared more inclusive than His followers.

One summer I began to re-examine these 'proof text' Scriptures for myself and found they were saying something completely different. For the last ten years I've been coming back to this same question: what *does* the Bible say about same-sex relationships and equal marriage? This book contains my 'workings out'.

Some will find my approach too conservative/ traditional. More out of habit, I still work from the New International Version (NIV) and use masculine pronouns for God (even though I know God is infinitely more than male.) Though a few urged me to cover polyamorous relationships, I do not feel I have the understanding or insight to do this (I won't judge what I do not understand.) However, others will think I've drifted from Biblical orthodoxy. Both criticisms are inevitable in our polarised times.

Language and definitions matter hugely. They are fluid and appropriated differently. For example, some see 'queer' as a dated term of abuse and yet today many within LGBTQ+ communities reclaim it with pride as an umbrella term for all those who are not cis heterosexual. I use it because others do.

I have served three fabulous churches: Altrincham Baptist Church, Chawn Hill Church, and now the growing community that is Chester Road Baptist Church. It seems we are becoming one of the most diverse churches in north Birmingham, at least in terms of age, ethnicity, gender, neuropathways, sexuality... It feels beautiful, challenging, important, messy, and hugely imperfect. We're a 'work in progress' (aren't we all?) and don't always agree with each other (why would we?). I have taught most of the content of this book through my Sunday ministry. This book brings it all together. That said, the views are my own.

I am grateful in particular to Rachel Conway-Doel, Luke Dowding, Revd Nik Hookey, Revd Justin Kennedy and others unnamed for their invaluable feedback on earlier drafts. Thanks also goes to Revd Dr Stephen Finamore, President of the Baptist Union (2024-25) and former Principal of Bristol Baptist College, for graciously agreeing to provide an alternative metanarrative. It's important 'conservative/ traditionalist' perspectives are understood, if not always shared.

I write in support of my LGBTQ+ siblings in Christ who have 'skin in the game': members of my church, colleagues in ordained ministry. Their voices and perspectives matter far more than mine. Too often this debate is had by 'professionals in collars'. I hope this book is helpful to a wider audience within our churches!

To inclusion *and beyond!*

Danny Brierley

1
Introduction

A pressing dilemma facing the Church is our attitude towards same-sex relationships. Should churches either accept and affirm LGBTQ+ – Lesbian, Gay, Bi-Sexual, Transgender, and Queer – people, or maintain a 'love the sinner but hate the sin' approach?

Having first been made a *criminal* offence punishable by death in 1533[1], homosexuality was only de-criminalised in England and Wales in 1967[2] (lesbian sex had never been criminalised). Change was initially slow. For example, the age of consent, that was criminalising LGBTQ+ youth and young adults, was only equalised in 2001[3] and it only became illegal to discriminate against gay, lesbian and bi-sexual people in the workplace in 2003.[4]

Mainstream British society has become increasingly more LGBTQ+ accepting. Equality legislation has afforded the same rights to gay people[5], including Civil Partnerships[6] and equal marriage.[7] Though there is still a long way to go, identifying as queer no longer carries the same social stigma or economic consequence it once did for many.

There is now strong pressure for the Church to follow the example of other sectors[8], like education, the health service, judiciary, and military, to conform to this changing social pattern, in both recognising and welcoming same-sex couples. Those outside the Church find it hard to understand why the Church can't simply modernise its beliefs. Consequently, the Church now finds itself marginalised and derided for its antiquated attitude to those who are LGBTQ+. Are we on the wrong side of history?

For sure, UK attitudes to same-same relationships have changed significantly. In 1983, 83% of all UK adults thought 'sexual relations between two adults of the same sex' was always, mostly, or sometimes wrong.[9] Just 17% thought such relationships "not wrong at all" (this fell further to 11% by 1987 due to fears about HIV/AIDS). Since then, this has dramatically reversed. By 2022, the percentage of UK adults who thought 'sexual relations between two adults of the same sex' was always, mostly, or sometimes wrong had fallen from 83% to 33%. That means the percentage of UK adults who thought 'sexual relations between two adults of the same sex' was "not wrong at all" had risen from 11% in 1987 to 67% in 2022. (During the Covid-19 'lockdown' it spiked even higher at 72%). Conversely, only 9% of UK adults think sexual relations between two adults of the same sex is "always wrong".

This societal shift will only increase as the generation factor works its way through. In 1983, just 3% of octogenarians thought sexual relations between two adults of the same sex "not wrong at all"; by 2022 that had risen to 46%. Those born in the 1990s are the most progressive, with 80% responding "not wrong at all". (That figure slipped to 71% for those born in the perhaps more polarised and online times in the Twenty First Century.) Society's objection to same-sex relationships is literally dying out. Those with no religion show even higher levels of support. The 2021 Census revealed that 9.3% of 16-24 year olds now identify as LGBTQ+, with the biggest increase for those who are bi-sexual (5.3%). There is an increasing divide between society and Church. A challenge that mustn't be ignored; those with lowest or no academic qualifications are far less tolerant (46%) than those with A 'levels (70%) or degrees (69%).

Research by YouGov[10] similarly finds that by 2023, 85% of Britons believe "same-sex relationships are just as valid as heterosexual relationships" (in 2012 it was 67%). What's more, 78% now support same-sex marriage (in 2011, it was only 42%).

During this same period, Church attendance has declined. In 1983, 66% of the British population identified as Christian; by 2018 it was down to 38%.[11] This decline is accelerating as older people – who were raised in more religious times and so have more established religious beliefs and church affiliations – are gradually being replaced by unaffiliated and non-religious younger people. They are the 'Nones' because, when asked about their religious affiliation or belief, they tick 'none'.

The Church's perceived negative attitude to same-sex attraction therefore presents a most significant barrier to mission and future church growth, particularly with younger generations. Perhaps as a generalisation (there will always be exceptions), particularly those aged under forty are incredulous that anyone or anything can still maintain discriminatory attitudes and practices. Certainly not an institution they would want to join. In previous decades many churches lost credibility when they struggled to take on board evolutionary understandings of Creation, preferring instead to hold to a literal interpretation of Six Day Creationism.[12] So, today, it seems the Church is threatened by another credibility gap – this time over its attitude to those who are LGBTQ+.

'Gen Z', those born between 1997 and 2012, are more progressive in their attitudes towards gender and sexuality than their parents, and even Millennials (those born, 1981-1996). For example, only 48% of 'Gen Z' believe there are just two genders, compared to 68% of over 25s.[13] And yet, dubbed YIPs, 'Young Illiberal Progressives', they are, paradoxically, also less tolerant of views they disagree with. How tragic that they should perceive the Church as oppressive and discriminatory. Of course, a feature of aging is often the gradual acceptance of nuance; the difference is, today's youth are starting from a place of acceptance. What does this say for the future of the Church, other than as a haven for the minority still uncomfortable with, or actively opposed to, LGBTQ+ inclusion?

Yet, the Church is not like other sectors. It's not just a complex human structure; it is the Body of Christ with God the Son as its Head [Col.1:18]. Therefore, the Church must not simply conform to the pattern of this world [Ro.12:2]. Just because 'the world' says something is acceptable, doesn't mean to God it *is* acceptable. Ultimately, the Church is answerable to God, as is society; this means having courage to be guided by the Spirit of Truth [Jn.16:3], not the 'spirit of the age'. For Christians, any opposition to or 'othering' of those who are lesbian, gay, bi, trans, queer or 'plus' – whether direct, indirect or institutional; subtle or in-your-face – that is not justified or called for by the Bible is nothing other than oppression – homophobia.

Of course, the flipside of this is that the Church must also be trans-formed by the renewing of its mind – continually. Then we will be able to test and approve what God's will is – His good, pleasing and perfect will [Ro.12:2]. For those in the Church, whether or not to accept and equalise LGBTQ+ people is not a social justice question (or even a mission/ church growth question); it is first and foremost a Bible question.

The question then becomes, so what <u>*does*</u> the Bible say about same-sex relationships and marriage?

I have a hunch: many Christians who oppose LGBTQ+ inclusion and same-sex marriage today do so because they think that's what they are *supposed* to believe. They want to be faithful to God and the Bible but rely on what others tell them the Bible says on the matter. Too many haven't properly read, let alone studied, it for themselves. What if it turns out they are defending a misunderstanding? What if the Bible says *more* than they thought, and yet does *not* say what they 've been told it says?

Engaging with the Bible

The Bible is by far the most published and yet least read – and even less understood – book of all time. Many people, religious and not, find strength, wisdom and inspiration from its content.

But it's more than a book. To be precise, it's a collection of 66 smaller books – the ultimate anthology – that, since the invention of the printing press in the sixteenth century, we've come to expect bound in one single volume. These 66 books were written over a spread of 1500 years by 40+ writers (mostly unknown to each other), drawn from three different continents, numerous cultures and languages, and written in a range of literary genres (historical accounts, legal statements, poetry and song lyrics, prophecies) to address a diverse range of local and historic issues of their day.

Compiled this way, the Bible is the Spirit-inspired, unfolding story of God and His people. Through it, we can trace a growing understanding and revelation of God through successive generations. Abraham may have been saved by faith [Heb.11:8-11] just as was Paul and yet, coming after the life, death and resurrection of Christ, surely Paul's understanding of God had greater clarity and definition than that of Abraham's.

But, again, the Bible is more than a book. For me, it carries the message of God. It's to be read and re-read, meditated on, spoken out in praise, studied, and even wrestled with. The Holy Spirit uses it to encourage, inspire and challenge me.

God could have provided a far shorter and concise book or even booklet – a bit like the UK Highway Code – that only required us to learn and do what it says, without much need for inspiration, interpretation, or questioning. Instead, God has given us a rich source of Scripture that forces us to think, pray, question, and debate. That's presumably why it contains *two* Creation narratives, *four* Gospels. The Holy Spirit leads us on a lifetime of discovery. We discover even greater depth and profound meaning when we investigate the historical contexts and cultural references, and appreciate its unity as we relate one part with another.

I say this simply to state the obvious: *the Bible requires interpreta-tion*. What we call 'hermeneutics' is all about the principles, method, and process of interpreting the Bible. When asked by an expert in the Scriptures (what we call the 'Old Testament'), Jesus replied, *"What is written in the*

Law? How do you read it?"[Lk.10:25-26]. He was asking, what's your 'take' on faith? How are you interpreting it? Jesus understood that Scripture has to be interpreted.

The Bible reveals a progression of understanding *within* its 66 books. For example, Apostle Peter was brought up the Jewish way, based on the Torah (Genesis-Deuteronomy) and the Prophets. He thought like a Jew, he acted like a Jew, he ate like a Jew. Then, one day, God told him through a dream to eat food strictly forbidden by Jewish laws, such as those contained in Leviticus chapter 11. Though initially repulsed, Peter had to revise his theology and practice in light of his new understanding. Leviticus had provided important insights (God was knowable and there were right and wrong ways to live) but then came greater clarity (further revelation): we don't and can't earn favour with God; He already delights in us anyway!

Now, the Scriptures might not change, but sometimes our interpretation of them does. The Bible may be infallible[14] to many Christians; our interpretation or reading of it is certainly not. A brief review of Church history confirms just how interpretations have been refined and clarified over the Centuries.

For example, the Church once taught the sun and all other planets and moons rotated around the Earth, which was said to be static. To be fair, that was the common understanding of the time.[15] Joshua 10:13, 1 Chronicles 16:30, Psalms 19:4-6, 93:1, 96:10, 104:5, 119:90 and Ecclesiastes 1:5 were quoted as evidence. But then Galileo Galilei (1564-1642) challenged this flawed interpretation, proving the Earth rotated around the sun. Galileo was charged with heresy and placed under house arrest for 24 years. But he was right! Today no-one seriously claims the sun rotates around the Earth. The Scriptures didn't change, but our interpretation of them did.

Some Christians used the Bible to justify slavery as God's social and global economic system. They cited Philemon, 1 Corinthians 7:21-24, Genesis 9:20-25, and Titus 2:9. Fortunately, other Christians, like Olaudah Equiano (1745-1797) and William Wilberforce (1759-1833), challenged this barbaric, evil and flawed interpretation. The Scriptures didn't change, but our interpretation of them did.

Other Christians supported apartheid in South Africa and racial segregation in the United States of America. Their reading or interpretation of the Bible (or at least selective verses from it) convinced them that God had ordained the supremacy of white people over all others. They cited Genesis 1 (they said Creation established a hierarchy of structures or 'orders'); Genesis 11 and again in Acts 2:5-11 (they said God had created and divided different races); Acts 17:26 (they said God had allocated different races into different spaces); Romans 13:1-7 (they said laws made by Government must be obeyed as God's authority). Now we look back with deep shame and repentance. Once more, the Scriptures didn't change, but our interpretation of them did.

Only a century ago some were using the Bible to oppose women's equal voting rights. Fifty years ago, many churches followed a 'male only' understanding of leadership. A decreasing minority still do. After all, didn't Apostle Paul say, *"I do not permit a woman to teach or to have authority over a man; she must be silent."* [1 Tim.2:12]? And that *"the women should keep silent in the churches."* [1 Cor.14:34]. And yet today its largely a settled issue, most Christians celebrating the leadership of women. The Scriptures haven't changed, but our interpretation has.

Likewise, there was a time when the Church gave little recognition to the work and ministry of the Holy Spirit. Then, 1960s youth culture emerged, and, with it, Christian young people re-read the book of Acts and 'discovered' what had always been in the Bible: that God the Holy Spirit empowers people with spiritual gifts.[16] Now many Christians today take this understanding for granted (and are baffled how previous generations could have missed what seems so obvious to them) but fifty years ago very few people read it that way. The Scriptures didn't change, but our interpretation of them did.

The Bible might not change, but our understanding or interpretation of it sometimes does. That's maybe why *"the word of God is alive and active.*

Sharper than any double-edged sword, it penetrates even to dividing soul and spirit, joints and marrow; it judges the thoughts and attitudes of the heart" [Heb 4:12]. The more we seek to *'know* this love', the more we recognise it *'surpasses* (at least, our) *knowledge'* [Eph.3:19]. There's a humility in recognising that, this side of 'completeness', 'now I know *in part;* then I shall know fully.' [1Co.13:10-12].

But how could this disparity of interpretations have arisen?

When watching TV, the picture – and our understanding of what's happening on the screen – is enhanced when we see all pixels in one go. If some pixels are omitted or others zoomed in on to the exclusion of all others, we get a distorted picture or understanding. So, I believe it is with the Bible. To get the fullest picture, we need to see all pixels (chapters and verses) in relation to each other.

I am an Evangelical[17] Christian who loves the Bible and who seeks to both better understand and better live it (not always as well as I might!) To gain a more complete picture or understanding, the Bible must be seen and understood in the whole, not in fragments.

However, I am not a 'fundamentalist' Christian.[18] For me, 'fundamentalists' *zoom in* on a few pixels or verses ('proof texts') of the Bible that support what they (already?) believe, to the exclusion of all others.

But neither am I a 'liberal' Christian.[19] For me, 'liberals' *omit* pixels or verses/ sections of the Bible they don't like or agree with and, in so doing, fail to grapple with the totality of Scripture. And, just like 'fundamentalist' Christians, 'liberals' therefore also fail to grapple with the totality of Scripture. Fundamentalists and liberals have more in common than they like to admit!

That's why, if I must have a label (other than simply as a follower of Jesus Christ), I prefer to be a *'progressive* evangelical'.[20] For me, it's not acceptable to simply omit sections of the Bible we don't like; but neither is it adequate to only zoom in on the bits we do like, whilst ignoring those bits that confuse or challenge our thinking. Luther (that's *Reformation* Luther, not *Vandross* Luther or *Detective* Luther) championed *Sola Scrip-*

ture – Scripture alone. He meant the whole of it, not just a few 'go-to' verses or 'proof text' pixels.

So, this exploration is unashamedly about digging deeper into the Bible. And, in particular, about examining what the Bible does and does not say about issues of sexuality and same-sex relationships.

I still read the same Bible, but now understand it slightly differently. I came to faith through, and spent my formative years in, 'conservative Evangelical' churches, both as a member and then on staff. Many years in, a fault line began to develop between what I was told God thought of gay people, and what I increasingly experienced God to be like. The Jesus I read about in the Gospels seemed more radically inclusive than His Church. I was struggling to reconcile the great doctrines of grace, justification by faith, and omnibenevolence with what seemed out-of-character Divine judgment directed at a minority group by the Church. In any case, if we're all 'dead to sin', why accuse some corpses of being more dead than others? Faced with similar questions, some walk away from faith; they no longer believe it. Others replace the questions with dogmatic statements (repeat them enough and they must be true). For me, it sent me back again and again to the Bible. That's a good thing, right?

What follows are my 'workings out': how I gradually came to affirm same-sex relationships and equal marriage – because of the Bible, not despite it. I'm very conscious that for many this is an 'issue', a debate about 'others'; whereas those who are LGBTQ+ have 'skin in the game' – it cuts to the core of their identity. I write and minister as an ally, standing in solidarity with my queer sisters and brothers in Christ.

It's important to acknowledge, most Christians who don't yet affirm LGBTQ+ inclusion and same-sex marriage, do so because of their high view of Scripture; not because they are homophobic. Charles Spurgeon (1834-1892) – hero to some, divisive to others – called on believers to have confidence and "uncage the lion"; to let the Bible speak for itself. He was adamant, *"The answer to every objection against the Bible is the Bible."*[21] So our task here is to 'uncage the lion' – always an unnerving experience!

Clearly, I am no Luther or Spurgeon, but I am part of a growing movement of evangelicals who are asking if our view of the Bible has been obscured by our inherited presuppositions, dogma, even pride. Far from being a 'downgrade', this is returning to the Scriptures and hearing them roar afresh. So, for my 'conservative/ traditionalist' brothers and sisters in Christ, I simply urge you to do what you do _so_ well: to keep digging deep into the Scriptures.

So, what does the Bible say?

The Bible doesn't say as much about same-sex identity as might be assumed from the volume of debate. A reading of the Bible cover to cover reveals there are _seven_ separate references made to homosexuality: four in the Old Testament and three in the New Testament. That's just under 0.02% of its entire content.

As an aside, the words 'homosexual' and 'homosexuality' didn't appear in any English translation of the Bible until the 1946 Revised Standard Version.[22] That's _not_ to suggest earlier translators didn't use substitute descriptions or words (they did), but the apparently clear and unambiguous language that some readers cite with such certainty from their modern translations was absent before then.

A 'liberal' Christian might say, just _omit_ these seven verses. Concentrate on the other 99.98%. If it helps your conscience, round up! Nevertheless, though few in number, these seven verses _are_ in the Bible and, therefore, to get the full picture, they can't simply be ignored. We must engage with them.

Likewise, a 'fundamentalist' Christian might say, _focus_ just on these seven verses. Concentrate on the 0.02%. Nevertheless, whilst these verses are undeniably included, so are the other 31,096 verses. For a more complete picture, we need to engage with the _whole_ of Scripture.

For many years, Christian objections to LGBTQ+ inclusion were based on these seven verses. 'The Bible _clearly_ says..', it was argued. Taking the

Bible seriously, we'll study these so called 'clobber passages'[23], and discover they aren't the 'smoking gun' some 'conservatives/ traditionalists' claim them to be. Interestingly, no longer able to cite these verses for their conservative polemic, many serious Biblicists have had to switch to alternative meta-narrative arguments to prop up their LGBTQ+ objections. To see why, let's first deal with these seven verses, beginning with the infamous story of Sodom and Gomorrah. Not only is it chronologically the first, it's also what those who don't know their Bibles most often fall back on.

> ### To think about...
>
> 1. Have you ever changed your mind about what the Bible says on an issue? What? Why? How?
>
> 2. How genuinely open are you to the possibility that the Bible may have more – even, different things – to say about sexuality than you currently realise?

2

Sodom! (And Gomorrah)

Genesis 19:1-5

*"**T**he two angels came to Sodom in the evening, and Lot was sitting in the gate of Sodom. When Lot saw them, he rose to meet them and bowed himself with his face to the earth and said, "My lords, please turn aside to your servant's house and spend the night and wash your feet. Then you may rise up early and go on your way." They said, "No; we will spend the night in the town square." But he pressed them strongly; so they turned aside to him and entered his house. And he made them a feast and baked unleavened bread, and they ate. But before they lay down, the men of the city, the men of Sodom, both young and old, all the people to the last man, surrounded the house. And they called to Lot, "Where are the men who came to you tonight? Bring them out to us, that we may know them."* Genesis 19:1-5

The chilling account of Sodom and Gomorrah in Genesis epitomises for many God's wrath towards queer people. Just look what happened: God judged and destroyed two whole cities, killing virtually all inhabitants, all on account of homosexual sin. Yet, the text reveals a different story to the caricature. Even *before* sending the two angels, and what happened to them, God had already decided to punish Sodom [Ge.13:13; 18:17]. The King James Version is coy: *"Bring them out unto us, that we may know them."* The New International Version is more upfront: *"Bring them out to us so that we can have sex with them."* But it's The Living Bible that is most direct: *"Bring out those men to us so we can rape them."* The application of this story changes the instant we realise it is *not* about same-sex attraction or sexual orientation, but about rape; on this occasion, male rape – male gang rape.[24]

Far from being judgmental, Abraham interceded on behalf of the people of Sodom and Gomorrah. Lot, Abraham's nephew, was providing all-important hospitality to two guests, angels sent by God. On discovering their presence, a local mob demanded that Lot hand his male guests over to be gang-raped by the male mob.

The story of Sodom and Gomorrah is not a judgment on two consenting members of the same gender having a faithful, life-long, committed, sexual relationship. The sin was *rape* - on this occasion, men raping men, gang rape. The mob wasn't expressing their love for, or attraction to, the two strangers; instead, their desire was to humiliate and break the human spirit. Rape and all forms of sexual violence are abhorrent. We shouldn't be surprised that God was angry with the mob.

The travesty is that sexual violence against women[25], as well as against men, has been condoned in many cultures and centuries (including our own). So important was the hospitality code, even Lot, whom Peter declared righteous [2Pe.2:7-8], appeared willing to offer up instead his own daughters to be raped by the male mob [Ge.19:8]. Inconsistently, those who see Sodom and Gomorrah as reason to oppose LGBTQ+ inclusion are not arguing for the rape of women. To compute that homosexual sex is inherently sinful because men raped men, we would also have to say that heterosexual sex is equally sinful because men rape women, just as David's sin of adultery (heterosexual unfaithful sex) with Bathsheba does not make all heterosexual expressions sinful.

Many Jewish commentators regard the sin of Sodom to be failing to practise hospitality. Abram and Sarai [Ge.18] and then Lot welcomed and provided for their strangers or angels [Ge.19], whereas the mob sought to humiliate and attack them. The Prophet Ezekiel spoke the word of the Lord, declaring, *"Now <u>this</u> was the sin of your sister Sodom: she and her daughters were arrogant, overfed and unconcerned; they did not help the poor and needy. They were haughty and did detestable things before me."* [Ezek.16:49-50]. Was this also what the writer to the Hebrews had in mind? *"Do not forget to show hospitality to strangers, for by so doing some people have shown hospitality to angels without knowing it"* [Heb.13:2]. It appears God didn't think the sin was consenting, monogamous, faithful same-sex relationships.

The story of Sodom and Gomorrah is a chilling reminder that sexual violence has been used to brutalise women and men for centuries. It was then – as now – totally abhorrent to God.

> ### To think about...
>
> 1. Read again Genesis 18:16-29. What do you notice this time? Be curious!
>
> 2. Why is the story of Sodom and Gomorrah so ingrained in our collective thinking?
>
> 3. Why is it taking so long to challenge sexual violence and the abuse of power?

What did the Law say?

For most Christians, Leviticus is not their 'go-to' book of the Bible. Its eclectic and, at times, obscure instructions can seem irrelevant. That is, until issues of sexuality arise.

Then, suddenly, Leviticus is championed for providing two of the seven verses in the Bible that appear to condemn those who are queer. After all, didn't Jesus declare *"I have not come to abolish the Law or the Prophets but to fulfil them. Anyone who breaks one of the least of these commandments and teaches others to do the same will be called least in the kingdom of heaven"* [Mt.5:17-20].

Except, Jesus wasn't calling for a return to a golden era of living by the Law. Instead, Jesus was radically reframing the Law, frequently saying, *"You have heard that it was said.. but I tell you..."* Jesus was calling people back into relationship with God, not conformity to a legal code.

Leviticus chapters 17-26 comprise what is often called the Holiness Code. This is a brief and rapid-fire succession of laws about right and wrong ways to live. Some argue they are an earlier text that was later inserted into Leviticus. For me, to avoid liberal or fundamentalist selectivity, we must engage with the whole of Scripture, including all of Leviticus. So, what's going on?

Whilst others at the time thought the forces of nature or 'gods' were distant, unknowable and aloof, the Book of Leviticus was a powerful statement that Yahweh, the One God, wants relationship with us. And that what we do affects our relationships with each other and ultimately with God. So, Leviticus has a profoundly important message.[26] We just need to be consistent in how we apply it.

If we condemn homosexuality, we must _also_ condemn the wearing of polyester shirts (mixing fibres was strictly forbidden) [Lv.19:19]; 'hipsters' with 'bed-head' hair [Lv.10:6], who wear ripped jeans [Lv.10:6], and have trimmed beards [Lv.19:27] and tattoos [Lv.19:28]. Leviticus declares all of these wrong. *And some!* Where would that leave our hipster worship leaders? We can't say, *this* law applies today, but *that* law doesn't, otherwise we risk relying on our own *likes* and *dislikes*, our own prejudices. For example, the Law also states a man who is found guilty of raping a young woman must be made to marry her, and with no option for later divorce [De.22:28-29]; no thought to the victim and her lifelong trauma of being forced to marry her rapist. Is anyone seriously suggesting this 'pixel of Scripture' must also be applied literally today? If no, then we are already acknowledging the need for interpretation and the need to see the Bible's full picture.

That said, some of the content in Leviticus was made obsolete by the destruction of the Temple in Jerusalem in AD 70. Some of its laws no longer apply because the situation they were addressing no longer exists. For example, requirements for the Temple-based Levitical priesthood and animal sacrifice. These were *fulfilled* (reframed, not abolished) by Christ, the Great High Priest. Even in Judaism the laws in Leviticus relating to the Temple and animal sacrifice are no longer considered applicable. (Ever wondered why modern-day Judaism doesn't perform animal sacrifices?) What else in Leviticus has Christ fulfilled (reframed)?

Conversely, there are many laws in Leviticus that we quietly overlook because they are uncomfortably challenging. They're an inconvenient truth we'd rather skip over. For example:

"If any of your fellow Israelites become poor and are unable to support themselves among you, help them as you would a foreigner and stranger, so that they can continue to live among you. Do not take interest or any profit from them, but fear your God, so that they may continue to live among you. You must not lend them money at interest or sell them food at a profit." Leviticus 25:35-37

Why are some laws considered redundant, but others considered still relevant? Who decides? And on what basis? Could it be we flawed 'sinners' have a tendency to declare as wrong ('sin') those things we see in others that we don't think apply to us?

Furthermore, when Leviticus appears to include two references to homosexuality, we mustn't *assume* that what we in the Twenty First Century understand by homosexuality is what the Scripture contributors and their Bible translators meant. Let's look at these two verses.

To think about...

1. How do you engage with the Book of Leviticus?

2. Mark Twain famously said, *"It ain't the parts of the Bible that I can't understand that bother me, it is the parts that I do understand!"*

3

Child abuse is an abomination

Leviticus 18:22

"Do not have sexual relations with a man as one does with a woman; that is detestable." Leviticus 18:22

The King James Version calls sex between two men an 'abomination', the NIV prefers 'detestable' (tov'evah); it's a thing that causes disgust or loathing. These strong words have led to so much mistreatment and self-loathing. How are we to understand this?

Leviticus 18 deals with a detailed and wide-ranging list of wrong unlawful practices, including:

- sex with a close family member (incest) [Lv.18:6-9];

- sex with a child (child abuse) [Lv.18:9-11];

- sex with a wider family member (adultery) [Lv.18:12-16];

- sex with more than one woman at the same time (group sex) [Lv.18:17]

- sex with more than one wife (bigamy) [Lv.18:18-20);

- child sacrifice (ritual abuse & infanticide) [Lv.18:21]

- sex between two men (homosexuality) [Lv.18:22];

- sex with an animal (bestiality) [Lv.18:23]

If this verse 22 'pixel' is to be taken literally, then:

1. Why does it only write from a *man's* perspective? Why would sex between two men be 'detestable' but sex between two women not?

2. Why were some 'Old Testament' individuals not condemned for breaking this Levitical code? For example, Jacob married his wife's sister [Ge.29]; Abraham married his half-sister [Ge.20:12]; Amram married his Aunt Jochebed [Ex.6:20]. If, as some argue, it was because the Law was not given to Moses until later. True, that suggests there *is* a gradual progression of understanding within the Bible of what is right and wrong. This process was only completed by Christ, hence why He would frequently say of the Law, *"You have heard that it was said.. But I tell you.."*

3. Why does it not say sex between a father and his daughter is also wrong? Some argue it was because it was so obvious, it didn't need saying. Yet, surely *"Don't have sex with your ox"* would have been even more obvious?! Others say, it *was* originally included but omitted in error by scribes. But, if they are saying the text is not complete, then what else needs correcting? To be consistent, anyone and everyone who 'committed' any of the above, would have to be "cut off from their people" [Lv.18:29].

4. There is debate about what v.22 is referring to:

   ○ Same-sex attraction (orientation)?

- ○ Same-sex sexually intimate activity?

- ○ Same-sex penetrative (anal) sex?

What some modern-day translators refer to as "sexual relations with a _man_" [Lv.18:22] is probably better understood as warning against "sexual relations with a _boy_". Jonathan Tallon, in his well-researched _Affirmative_, notes the deliberate linguistic distinction between 'male' and 'woman'[27]. What is being condemned is child abuse; that is, sex with a minor, a young boy. Remember, translating into English ancient Hebrew texts written thousands of years ago is not a precise science. The Ancient Hebrew-speakers didn't leave us Google Translate or the Oxford English-Ancient Hebrew Dictionary.

> "_Do not give any of your **children** to be sacrificed to Molek, for you must not profane the name of your God. I am the Lord. Do not have sexual relations with a **man** as one does with a woman; that is detestable._"

A better understanding is:

> "_Do not give any of your **children** to be sacrificed to Molek, for you must not profane the name of your God. I am the Lord. Do not have sexual relations with a **boy** as one does with a woman; that is detestable._"

Verses 21 and 22 are both condemning the same thing – child sacrifice and child abuse. Who doesn't condemn that? Chapter 18 begins and ends with an important challenge to live both differently and better than other societies. Consequently, whilst others may get drawn into incest, bigamy, child abuse and child sacrifice, God's people are to be different. In an age when we are having to face up to historic child abuse within the Church and other institutions, Leviticus 18 is a powerful and sobering call for us to live differently and better.

What the NIV translates as 'detestable' and the King James Version calls an 'abomination', might be easier understood today as a 'taboo': that being, what is generally understood by all to be socially, morally, ethically wrong. If so, what constitutes a 'taboo' can change with time and place. 'Breaking a taboo' is unthinkable at the time, and yet, some (by no means all) taboos don't stand the test of time. Women wearing "men's clothing" and men wearing "women's clothing" [De.22:5] is similarly 'detestable' (NIV), an abomination (KJV) or 'taboo' [Dt.22:5], and yet one man's Braveheart *kilt* is wearing your sister's *skirt*.

To think about...

1. If we are selective about which Levitical laws should be applied today, what does that say about us?

2. Why historically has the Church been slow to address child abuse but quick to condemn LGBTQ+ people?

3. If you were persistently told you are an abomination or detestable to God, what effect might this have on you and your mental health?

4

Death penalty?

Leviticus 20:13

"If a man has sexual relations with a man as one does with a woman, both of them have done what is detestable. They are to be put to death; their blood will be on their own heads." Leviticus 20:13

If Leviticus 18 lists unlawful sexual *practices*, Leviticus 20 describes their *punishments*. As with Leviticus 18, Leviticus 20 starts by making clear the context is *child abuse* and child sacrifice (ritual abuse and infanticide) [Lv.20:1-5].

"Any Israelite or any foreigner residing in Israel who sacrifices any of his children to Molek is to be put to death." Leviticus 20:1

It is to be death by stoning [Lv.20:2]. Moses then warns of the severe consequences for 'turning a blind eye' to such child abuse and child sacrifice [Lv.20:4-5]. There is to be no cover-up, no quietly transferring someone's ministry to another region or diocese.

If this verse [Lv.20:13] is to be taken literally and applied today, then all men (again, no mention of women) who have a same-sex intimate relationship should not only be condemned, they should be stoned to death (a form of execution that relies on mob violence). Tragically, LGBTQ+ people have been persecuted and oppressed for all generations. In some areas of the world, LGBTQ+ people are still being stoned to death. Western society rightly condemns such barbarism (though not enough to jeopardise economic interests.) And yet, LGBTQ+ people still face violence and intimidation in the UK. Sexual orientation hate crimes in England and Wales rose by 41% to 26,152, according to Home Office data for the year ending March 2022 – the largest annual percentage increase since records began in 2012.[28] Similarly, transgender identity hate crimes also increased by 56% to 4,355. For example, on 11th February 2023 sixteen-year-old Brianna Ghey was brutally murdered, stabbed 28 times.[29] She was transgender and had a substantial TikTok following. Sections of the media were later criticised for 'deadnaming' her.[30] It's not enough to debate inclusion; it's literally 'life and death' for some. Intimidation and violence towards gay people – done in the name of God – is leading to higher rates of self-harm among gay people and shames both society and Church alike.

Of course, with religious extremist exceptions, Christians who don't yet feel able to affirm LGBTQ+ people are not calling for the death penalty; simply asserting that homosexual sex is wrong and to be condemned as sin. Curiously, by *not* calling for the death penalty, they are acknowledging that the Levitical text should *not* be taken literally and *does* require interpretation!

Furthermore, if this verse [Lv.20:13] is to be applied today, then it's not just gay couples that must be stoned to death. To be consistent, so too must anyone who has ever done any chores on a Sunday [Nu.15:32-36] or cursed one of their parents [Lv.20:9] – no mention of provocation as an excuse! And any man or woman (so earlier omissions of women were not accidental?) who is a medium or spiritualist [Lv.20:27]. We'd need a lot more stones! Of course, no-one thinks we should be doing that.

Other reasons to stone people to death include, if a *man* is caught *having* sexual relations with an animal (bestiality) [Lv.20:15]. The animal (non-consenting victim), it says, must also be put to death. However, if a _woman_ is said to be _approaching_ an animal for sex, she and the animal must be stoned to death. How many times in a male-dominated, agricultural society must this have been conveniently cited to perniciously and falsely accuse and conveniently put to death an innocent woman on the pretence she had gone *near* an animal 'obviously with a sexual intent'? Doesn't only God know the true motives of the heart?

Leviticus is a much-misunderstood book with a profoundly important message today about the potential for relationship with God and the effects our behaviours can have on both each other and God. But Leviticus does _not_ provide the clear condemnation of gay couples in a 'til death us do part' committed relationship that some claim it does.

To think about...

1. Why don't we stone to death those who do chores on a Sunday or curse their parent? Why is fixating on 'pixels' sometimes dangerous?

2. Why don't we stone to death all gay couples?

3. Why are LGBTQ+ people still subjected to violence? How can we end this? Where does this violence stem from?

5

Gang rape?

Judges 19

"While they were enjoying themselves, some of the wicked men of the city surrounded the house. Pounding on the door, they shouted to the old man who owned the house, 'Bring out the man who came to your house so we can have sex with him.' The owner of the house went outside and said to them, 'No, my friends, don't be so vile. Since this man is my guest, don't do this outrageous thing." Judges 19:22-23

If ever there was a chapter in the Bible that requires interpretation it is Judges 19. Read it now!

A rural priest (a Levite) was having a 'not-so-secret' *affair* with a woman[31]. After a while, the priest thought his *lover* was being unfaithful – *to him*. The priest was outraged! She left him and returned to her parent's home. Some translations say, far from being unfaithful to the priest, she was *fearful* of him[32]. Four months later the priest tried to get her back. On arrival at her parents' home, his ex-lover's father insisted the priest stay for one, then two, three, and finally four nights. Whatever the father thought about the priest, he put aside in order to offer this stranger the all-important 'hospitality code'. Eventually the priest set off for Jerusalem with his now reunited lover. And his servant. And his two donkeys. Getting dark, the servant suggested they stop the night in Jerusalem, then controlled by the Jebusites. Being full of 'people *not* like us', the priest kept going until the safety of Gibeah and 'people like us'. But 'the people like us' did not offer them any hospitality. They were left sitting in the town square.

Eventually an old man living in Gibeah, but who was from the same rural area as the priest, invited them to stay with him. Again, that all-important 'hospitality code'. He asked the priest: *'Where are you going?'* and *'Where have you come from?'* How would we answer these profound questions (in relation to our attitudes to same-sex attraction and acceptance)?

But then some local men surrounded the house, pounded on the door and demanded the old man send out his guest so that the mob could have sex with him. *What?* The old man says their behaviour is vile and disgraceful. *Baam!* So, homosexuality is vile and disgraceful. It's Sodom and Gomorrah all over again.

Except the male mob isn't proposing a consensual, faithful, life-long same-sex relationship with the priest. They've never met him before; most don't even know what he looks like. This is indeed similar to 'Sodom and Gomorrah'. Again, it's about rape, men raping men, gang rape; using sexual violence to brutalise, dehumanise and humiliate another person, leaving them in no doubt of their powerlessness. It's using sexual violence to break the human spirit.

The old man was faced with a horrid dilemma. Who should he protect, his own 'flesh and blood' or the strangers he had only met a few hours ago? He knew what the mob were capable of. Through Western eyes the assumption is 'look after your own' first, and then – only if it's possible and safe to do so – assist the strangers. But this isn't the West, it's the East. And the all-important 'hospitality code' says, no matter what the cost or risk, welcome and treat strangers as if they are your own flesh and blood. So, the old man was faced with an impossible decision: hand over his own 'flesh and blood' to the mob or hand over his own 'flesh and blood' to the mob. Either way, he'd blame himself for the rest of his life.

So, he handed his own 'flesh and blood' over to the mob. And they raped her. They repeatedly gang-raped the priest's lover throughout the night. Sickening. It's the same male mob who had earlier wanted to rape the priest. It wasn't that they were sexually attracted to the priest, they simply wanted to use sexual violence to break these 'strangers'.

When morning came, the mob let her go. Somehow, she managed to make it back to the house. But life was ebbing from her. She died in the doorway – alone – from the brutal and prolonged sexual assaults.

How could such an horrific crime have happened? Judges 19 opens with, *"In those days Israel had no king"* [Jud.19:1]. There was a total breakdown in civic society. No government, No rule of law. It was pure anarchy. The scene of a 'Mad Max' film.

The priest, who had clearly known his lover had been taken by the mob, had evidently gone to bed. Worse, in the morning, he went to leave the old man's house *and his lover* to continue his journey north. (Just what had he professed to her back at her parents' house that had convinced her to return to him?) And now he was abandoning her. But his exit was blocked by her _dead_ body in the doorway. Even the priest couldn't ignore this. Who knows what went through his mind? He put her lifeless body on his donkey and took her back to his rural home.

Having travelled days with his lover's *dead* body and goodness knows what thoughts and emotions, on bringing her home, he dismembered her body - limb by limb. He then put together twelve parcels of body parts and sent them to the twelve tribes (extended families) across Israel. Logistically, how did he achieve that? No FedEx. So, either he sent servants out to walk the special deliveries or he embarked on a prolonged and very dark period of his life making the hand deliveries himself, one by one, over months, possibly years.

Today we understand more about the psychological trauma caused by horrific incidents. PTSD – Post Traumatic Stress Disorder. We see it in battle-hardened combat troops that struggle to adjust outside of the war zone. Was the priest suffering from PTSD? Or did the priest suffer from an undiagnosed dangerous personality disorder?

What of those who received the parcels? They were horrified. Shock turned to anger when they discovered what had happened to the priest's lover. Made even worse (if that's possible) by the fact that the rapist murderers were members of one of their fellow tribes of Israel. This had been done by 'people like us' – some of their own.

What then followed escalated into a brutal, all-out civil war with the slaughter of tens of thousands of people. And, when the last battle had been fought and the offending tribe of Benjamin destroyed, the eleven remaining tribes were left ruminating the needless loss of their fellow tribe; there were now eleven tribes when there should have been twelve. Futility.

Yes, this is a deeply troubling story about the vile and disgraceful behaviour of some men. What it is *not* is evidence that God condemns consensual, faithful, lifelong 'until death us do part' same-sex relationships. It's another stark reminder that sexual violence, be that towards women or men, has been part of our humanity's shameful past *and will continue to be so* until we as a society learn something of the 'hospitality code'.

To think about...

1. Why is this incident in the Bible?

2. Why have LGBTQ+ people experienced violence – physical, emotional, psychological, spiritual – from the Church?

3. Regarding your thinking about sexuality, where are you going? Where have you come from?

What did Jesus say?

Let me be very clear, I believe and uphold every single word Jesus said about same-sex relationships.

Jesus said..

.. nothing.

Jesus said _nothing_ about same-sex relationships.

At least not directly and not that Matthew, Mark, Luke or John thought worth recording.

More later.

6

It ain't natural?

Romans 1:26-28

"For this reason, God gave them up to dishonourable passions. For their women exchanged natural relations for those that are contrary to nature; and the men likewise gave up natural relations with women and were consumed with passion for one another, men committing shameless acts with men and receiving in themselves the due penalty for their error. And since they did not see fit to acknowledge God, God gave them up to a debased mind to do what ought not to be done." Romans 1:26-28

For someone who speaks so much about grace and inclusivity, Paul is still often caricatured as a misogynist, anti-women, homophobic, anti-gay. Part of the evidence for this is the appearance – and their interpretation – of three statements he apparently made about homosexuality.

Of all the 'clobber verses', the reference in Romans has become the centrepiece of conservative objections to LGBTQ+ inclusion. Not surprisingly, there are several different ways to understand what Paul might have been saying, and why.

First, what did Paul understand by *natural* and *unnatural* relations? What one considers *natural*, another might perceive as quite *unnatural*. Was Paul addressing Stoic attitudes to sex? He had certainly rubbed up against this sect before [Ac.17:18] and used familiar language to engage them. In the ancient Greek world, Stoic philosophy taught that the Divine was in the natural order, and that this was revealed through Reason. It was the task of all to conform to the patterns set within nature and, crucially, to avoid any, and all, distractions of pleasure. They shunned fun! This necessitated virtuous living and self-control over the 'passions of the flesh'. They believed sex was strictly for reproduction (procreation), not for pleasure; it was a duty, not something to be enjoyed. For Stoics, sex was *natural* if, and only if, it led to conception; anything else was considered *unnatural*.

The ancient world that Paul was addressing knew nothing of what is now widely accepted: that sexuality is an *orientation* (part of the natural order), not just a learnt or chosen behaviour (nurture). They assumed *everyone* was biologically attracted to the opposite sex. Had they known that some are *born* gay, they would have realised, a gay person would have 'exchanged natural relations' if they had gone against their natural orientation and had sex with someone of the opposite sex. As unnatural as it is for a 'straight' person to have gay sex, so it is for a gay person to have 'straight' sex. They would be exchanging or giving up their natural relations for opposite-sex attraction. Neither Paul nor the God-inspired Scriptures got it wrong because neither were speaking about what we understand today as sexual orientation, and faithful, monogamous, "till death us do part" same-sex relationships.

Similarly, today, we have better understanding of neuropathways. Whilst most people, by definition, are neuro-*typical*, a minority are neuro-*divergent*; their brains perceive, process and interact with the world slightly differently to others. This includes those ascribed labels as Attention Deficit Hyperactivity Disorder (ADHD), Autism Spectrum Condition (ASC), Dyspraxia, and Dyslexia. Whilst previous generations, through a combination of ignorance, fear, and intolerance, viewed such people as being in *deficit* (as if there is something *wrong* with them), we've come to realise it's about their *difference*, not *deficit*. We don't tell an autistic person to cease, exchange, confess, or seek a cure for their ASC traits.[33] We appreciate this is their *natural* way, how they've been 'wired' from birth – it's their 'normal'. No better, no worse than the majority – just different! Instead, we celebrate the God-gift they – and their autism – are to humanity. They, like everyone else, are equally made in the image of God [Ge.1:27]. We want those who are neuro-divergent to be able to say, as surely as those who are neuro-typical, *"I praise you because I am fearfully and wonderfully made; your works are wonderful, I know that full well."* [Ps.139:14]. So, why would we treat those whose sexual orientation is *different* to the majority as a deficit?

It's an important question because there is growing evidence that a sizeable contingent of autistic people are also lesbian, gay, bi or trans, when compared to 'straight' people. Some research finds as much as 18% of ASC men and 43% of ASC women may also be LGBTQ+.[34] If this is their 'normal' – how they have been created in God's image – then who are we to judge them as unnatural?

For others, sexual desire and romantic feelings are anything but 'natural'. Those who identify around asexuality – a broad umbrella term based on attraction, not behaviour – have persistent low to no interest in having sex (asexual) or an intimate emotional relationship (aromantic). That said, some may occasionally have sex: to accommodate their partner's need; functionally, to get pregnant; or only if they've established an exclusive emotional bond – without that they experience *no* sexual attraction or desire (demisexual).[35] Being asexual (or one of its micro-labels) is not a lifestyle choice (like celibacy), an absence of opportunity (like being single), or the result of an emotional/ psychological deficit (trauma); it's their queerness, the sexual orientation they were born with. It can't therefore be 'exchanged'. Whilst less than 1% of the adult population identify as asexual,[36] it's much more common for those who are autistic.[37]

When 'A' is added to 'LGBTQ+', George and Stokes (2018)[38] find that 70% of autistic people identify as lesbian, gay, bi, trans, queer, or asexual (LGBTQA+), and only 30% as cis heterosexual. This may be because those who are autistic often appear less reliant on social norms and so more willing to express their individuality. After all, didn't Paul say, *"Do not conform to the pattern of this world"* [Ro.12:2]?

Second, Paul was paraphrasing, even parodying, the way many Greek-influenced Jews 'demonised' 'Gentiles' (all those who weren't born Jewish), circulating stories about how vile they were. We see how some ethnic or social groups are 'demonised' today. That's why, after starting with praise for *'us/you'*, Paul then contrasts this by frequently referring to *'they/them'*. There is an *'us'* and *'them'*. Until – bam – in Romans 2:1 he flips it. Paul's point all along was *not* about what the Gentiles might or might not do or how bad they were. Instead, Paul was calling all people (and 'believers' who should have known better) to a non-judgmental way – the Jesus way.

Third, Paul appears to have been referencing Leviticus 20:13.

Leviticus 20:13	Romans 1:27
Statement of the act:	Statement of the act:
"If a man has sexual relations with a man as one does with a woman"	"In the same way the men also abandoned natural relations with women and were inflamed with lust for one another."
Comment on the act:	Comment on the act:
"both of them have dome what is detestable."	"Men committed shameful acts with other men"
Consequences of the act:	Consequences of the act:
"They are to be put to death; their blood will be on their own heads."	"and received in themselves the due penalty for their error."

When Jesus said, *"You have heard that it was said.. but I tell you..",* He was *not* contradicting the *Scriptures*; He *was* correcting the *religious elite's* distorted *interpretations.* The Pharisees had a 'glass half-empty' view of God. Believing God angry, they aimed to keep Israelites on the right side of God. Instead, Jesus showed that God was radically *for* people, especially those the religious elite labelled 'sinners'. When quoting Scripture, Jesus sometimes subtly shifted its focus. For example, when quoting Isaiah 53 (the 'suffering servant passage), Jesus included the first part of v.4, *"He took up our infirmities and carried our sorrows"* [Isa.53:4a; Mt.8:17] but chose not to include the second half, *"Yet we considered him stricken by God, smitten by him, and afflicted"* [Isa.53:4b].[39]

In Romans 1 Paul appears to have used the same approach. He quoted from Leviticus 20:13 but dropped the call for execution of homosexuals. Some say Paul only removed the death penalty to make it easier for the church in Rome to 'submit to the governing authorities' [Ro.13:1-5], because Rome tolerated homosexuality. It's more likely Paul was simply following Christ's example in calling people to be merciful and generous to all – even to those previously 'demonised'. If Paul was condemning gay women, with their "unnatural relations" (nowhere else prohibited in the Bible), he would have been going further than the Levitical Law, which made no mention of women. If his intent had been to uphold that under-standing of the Law, it would seem inconsistent of him to have dropped the death penalty for gay men?

Fourth, the insertion of chapters and verses in the Bible came 1500 years after Christ[40]. Deciding where one chapter ends and the next starts is a matter of *interpretation.* Does one sentence conclude the last point or introduce the next? So, Paul wraps up his parody by declaring, "Therefore" (Διὸ, dio)[41]:

**"You, therefore, have no excuse, you who pass judgment
on someone else, for at whatever point you judge anoth-**

***er, you are condemning yourself, because you who
pass judgment do the same things." Romans 2:1***

The emphasis changes when Romans 2:1 is seen as a continuum of Romans 1. Paul's point was 'don't judge' (ironically opposite to how some apply Romans 1). We shouldn't be surprised that there are no quotation marks in the text. Again, Bible translators haven't used quotation marks because ancient Greek didn't have such punctuation and Paul was paraphrasing their sentiment, not reciting an exact quote.

Paul was demonstrating that neither the Gentiles, with their fertility cults in Romans 1, nor the Jews with their strict legalism in Romans 2, had the full understanding of God. Paul was building up to say 'ALL people (Gentiles and Jews, male and female, black and white, straight and gay, young and old... Keep going – ALL people) have sinned' [Ro.3:23] and ALL [those same ALL people] find justification through Christ. It's because of who Christ is and what He has done (not who we are and what we have done.) That's why it's grace.

It's important to say, Paul was NOT giving people licence to do whatever they like with whoever they like, whenever they like. Hedonism, lawlessness, and sexual impurity are *not* condoned in Christian discipleship. ALL people, whether attracted to the opposite sex or same sex, are called to pursue sexual purity. Whether 'straight', 'gay' or 'bi', sex belongs within the commitment, faithfulness, and exclusivity of relationship between two people.

Regarding this, those who are bisexual have often been misrepresented: they've been seen as too queer and labelled promiscuous by some who are 'straight', and yet not queer enough by some lesbian and gay siblings for not having fully 'come out'. However, bisexuality is principally an orientation, not a behaviour. Someone who is 'bi' can be fulfilled in an exclusive heterosexual partnership just as someone who is straight can be unfulfilled. Our orientation may be determined from birth, but we spend a lifetime growing in self-awareness of who we are as God has formed us.

If bisexuality is sexual attraction to both your own and one other gender (historically, to both men and women), pansexuality sees beyond gender identity to be sexually attracted to a person, whatever gender you or they may be. There is something refreshingly innocent and affirming about being 'pan': simply loving someone for who they are, not because of the label others have assigned them. As God said to Samuel the priest about David: *"People look at the outward appearance, but the Lord looks at the heart"* [1Sa.16:7]. Regardless of our gender or identity, be that straight, gay, bi, pan, or whatever, sex belongs within the commitment, faithfulness, and exclusivity of relationship between two people.

Back to Romans, Paul wrote, *"Because of this, God gave them over to shameful lusts"* [Ro.1:26]. Who are the "them" that Paul is referring to? He says:

> *"They have become filled with every kind of wickedness, evil, greed and depravity. They are full of envy, murder, strife, deceit and malice. They are gossips, slanderers, God-haters, insolent, arrogant and boastful; they invent ways of doing evil; they disobey their parents; they have no understanding, no fidelity, no love, no mercy. Although they know God's righteous decree that those who do such things deserve death, they not only continue to do these very things but also approve of those who practise them."* Romans 1:29-32

This is strong language. Was Paul seriously suggesting this best and uniquely describes those who today identify as LGBTQ+? Think of those you know! In any case, Paul says, these *men* had relationships with *women* [v.27]. Instead, it's quite possible Paul was instead referring to the inner court of Rome. Emperor Nero, and his predecessor, Gaius Caesar Augustus Germanicus, known as Caligula or 'little boot', were tyrants who ruled with fear and utter depravity. Paul wouldn't have named "them", for fear of reprisal, but his readers would have made the connection.

Similarly, Paul had written:

> **"Although they knew God, they neither glorified him as God nor gave thanks to him, but their thinking became futile and their foolish hearts were darkened. Although they claimed to be wise, they became fools and exchanged the glory of the immortal God for images made to look like a mortal human being and birds and animals and reptiles. Therefore God gave them over in the sinful desires of their hearts to sexual impurity for the degrading of their bodies with one another. They exchanged the truth about God for a lie, and worshipped and served created things rather than the Creator – who is for ever praised. Amen."** *Romans 1:21-25*

Again, it hardly seems proportionate to single out lesbian, gay, bi, or trans people for such rebuke. And what's with the dressing up as animals or birds? Surely this is a reference to idolatrous temple practices. Remember, Paul was writing to the church in Rome. Then, Rome had the biggest temple to pagan gods, where temple prostitutes - male slaves - were castrated and 'given' to the temple to generate its income. They were human-trafficked sex-slaves. Paul was not condemning the slave victims (who would?); Paul was strongly condemning those who, by buying sex from the trafficked temple sex slaves, were sustaining that oppressive system. Still today, victims of sexual assault or sex trafficking are sometimes blamed or penalised, rather than the perpetrators.

Maybe Paul was also challenging unfaithful, non-monogamous sex. Was he speaking out against those who 'exchange' (swap) their sexual partners? Was he warning against risky sexual behaviours involving multiple sexual partners? After all, the men and women Paul refers to, *abandoned* (implying, it was their choice) 'natural relations' (their normal sexual attraction) with the opposite gender for sex with those of the same gender. It is their lustful and promiscuous behaviour with multiple partners that Paul is challenging, not their sexual orientation *per se*. That's why he refers to lust, but not love or faithfulness.

To think about...

1. How do you define 'natural'? What for you is 'normal'?

2. If _all_ have 'sinned', why do some Christians, consciously, or subconsciously, grade 'gay sinners' worse than 'straight sinners'? If _all_ have sinned, why all the focus on queer people?

7

Sex trafficking and Temple prostitution?

1 Corinthians 6:9-11a

"Or do you not know that the wicked will not inherit the kingdom of God? Do not be deceived: neither the sexually immoral, nor idolaters, nor adulterers, nor male prostitutes nor homosexual offenders, nor thieves, nor the greedy, nor drunkards, nor slanderers, nor swindlers will inherit the kingdom of God. And that is what some of you were." 1 Corinthians 6:9-11a

Paul gave examples of those who won't inherit the Kingdom of God. To be consistent, we mustn't separate the 'sexually immoral' and the 'men who have sex with men' from the greedy, those who drink too much, those who speak unfairly of others, and those who manipulate the system for their own financial gain. Here it says thieves won't inherit the Kingdom of God and yet Jesus told one of the robbers being crucified, *"I tell you the truth, today you __will__ be with me in Paradise"* [Mt.27:38; Mk.15:27;

Lk.23:32-43]. In any case, aren't we saved because of Christ and what He has done, not because of our own merits? Whatever Paul was saying, it was not simply to condemn LGBTQ+ people.

It was common in Greco-Roman culture for men to assert their power by holding dinner parties in pagan temples. These would include sacrifices to the gods, over-indulgence of food and alcohol, culminating in sexual orgies with temple prostitutes (both male and female). Paul was calling out such excessive and abusive behaviour; he was not making a comment about consensual, faithful, exclusive same-sex relationships. Similarly, Peter reminded his readers of their past lifestyles: *"You have spent enough time in the past doing what pagans choose to do – living in debauchery, lust, drunkenness, orgies, carousing and detestable idolatry" [1Pe.4:3]*. Like Peter, Paul was not referring to consensual, faithful, monogamous same-sex relationships.

Translating from Ancient Greek into English (or any other language) requires interpretation. For example, what the USA edition of the NIV translates as "men who have sex with men", the NIV's UK edition translates as *"male prostitutes nor homosexual offenders", whereas the RSV translates as "sexual perverts"*. Then the KJV comes in with *"nor effeminate, nor abusers of themselves with mankind"*. What, for the RSV, makes someone a 'sexual pervert'? What one heterosexual married couple might consider sexual perversion (not 'their cup of tea') might be another heterosexual consenting married couple's more expressive and varied sex life. Likewise, what, for the KJV, makes someone 'effeminate' (what it translates μαλακοὶ, malakoi, as)? That's full of cultural subjectivity. Today, male grooming is increasingly the 'norm'; more men are waxing, moisturising, or concealing to attract women, not other men. Are they all being 'effeminate' (malakoi)?

In Bible translators' defence, not only must they do their vital work without Google Translate, they must also contend with Paul's habit of creating his own terminology. Language evolves. New words and phrases are emerging all the time. We all know and love brunch (later and bigger than breakfast but earlier and smaller than lunch) and we all got very polarised over Brexit (Britain + exit) but did you know that to skitch, blending skate/ski and hitch, refers to holding on to a moving motor vehicle whilst on a skateboard or bicycle? Now that skitch is officially in the English dictionary, how do you translate it into French?

In the same way, Paul sometimes created new language, merging two words to form one new word.[42] Here, in 1 Corinthians 6 (and in 1 Tim.1:10-11), he merged the ancient Greek words ἄρσην ('male') and κοίτης ('bed') to make ἀρσενοκοίτης (*arsenokoítēs*). He wasn't referring to a literal 'male bed' (as if a bed has a gender). So, what did he mean?

Today, the NIV puts together *'malakoi'* and *'arsenokoítēs'* to make *"men who have sex with men"*. What's more, in a footnote that reveals the translators' predisposition, it claims this "refers to the passive and active participants in homosexual acts." The 1984 edition preferred, *"nor male prostitutes nor homosexual offenders."* Paul was once again condemning the practice of male prostitution and temple sex slaves. The NIV translators were making a distinction between the victims (male prostitution/ temple sex slaves) and the offenders (those who support and encourage such sex trafficking by purchasing sex with male sex slaves). In his ground-breaking 1534 Geneva translation, Reformation hero Martin Luther translated *arsenokoítēs* as 'knabenschänder' or 'boy molester', based on 'knaben'/boy and 'schänder'/molester. Luther clearly thought Paul was condemning pederasty (a sexual relationship between an adult man and a boy, often a young slave.)

Paul's big point wasn't to label some people worse than others; it was that, whilst we <u>ALL</u> have the potential to 'mess up' – to deceive and be deceived – in different ways [Ro.3:23], we ALL have the same opportunity to be sanctified, justified because its ultimately <u>ALL</u> about what Christ does, and His Spirit within us; not what we do. So, 1 Corinthians 6:9-11 says:

*"Or do you not know that the wicked will not inherit the kingdom of God? Do not be deceived: neither the sexually immoral, nor idolaters, nor adulterers, nor male prostitutes nor homosexual offenders, nor thieves, nor the greedy, nor drunkards, nor slanderers, nor swindlers will inherit the kingdom of God. And that is what some of you were. **But you were washed, you were sanctified, you were justified in the name of the Lord Jesus Christ and by the Spirit of our God.**"*

Again, Paul *was* warning against sexual immorality, but it's far from clear he was condemning faithful, monogamous same-sex relationships.

To think about...

1. To what extent do we still blame and shame the victims of sex trafficking and prostitution?

2. Why and how does power corrupt, even in religious settings?

8

Practising homosexuals?

1 Timothy 1:10-11

"..for the sexually immoral, for those practising homosexuality, for slave traders and liars and perjurers, and for whatever else is contrary to the sound doctrine that conforms to the gospel concerning the glory of the blessed God, which he entrusted to me." 1 Timothy 1:10-11

As in 1 Corinthians 6:9-11, Paul here again used his new word ἀρσενοκοίτης (arsenokoítēs) formed from the two other words ἄρσην ('male') and κοίτης ('bed'). But what did he mean? Though more recent Bible versions have translated ἀρσενοκοίτης (arsenokoítēs) as 'homosexuality', given that the notion of sexual orientation as a social construct did not first appear until the mid-nineteenth century, it seems unlikely Paul was referring to what is currently understood as homosexuality. The UK edition of the NIV Bible simply translates it as *"for adulterers and perverts, for slave traders..."*

Incidentally, those who use ἀρσενοκοίτης (arsenokoítēs) to refer to all gay people – men and women – have already strayed from the Biblical text because here Paul only referred to men (not women). To suggest 1 Timothy 1:10-11 includes lesbian couples is to go beyond the text.

First, Paul is making a broad point about the Law. NT Wright[43] thinks Paul was linking 'law breakers and rebels' to the Ten Commandments [Ex.20:1-17].[44] Paul included those who kill their fathers or mothers (the extreme opposite of honouring parents, the 5th Commandment); murderers (6th Commandment); adulterers and perverts (all kinds of non-married sexual activity, 7th Commandment); slave traders (an extreme form of stealing, 8th Commandment); liars and perjurers (9th Commandment) and the catch-all 10th Commandment. So, when Paul referred to 'adulterers and perverts' (which some Bible translators conflate with 'homosexuality'), Paul was making a broader point: whilst sex outside of marriage in all its forms is just another example of unhealthy behaviour, it is the gospel (the radical good news) of Jesus – not the law – that reveals God's glory.

Second, in referring to *"the sexually immoral, for those practising homosexuality, for slave traders,"* Paul was again speaking out against the practice of male temple prostitution, men who sleep with them, and the slave dealers who procure them (just as 1 Cor.6). Paul had left Timothy in charge of the church in Ephesus. This was one of the largest cities in the Roman Empire and home to the Temple of Artemis, one of the 'seven wonders of the world'. The Temple was used to worship the fertility goddess known by the Greeks as Artemis and by the Romans as Diana. Sexual intercourse was seen as a re-enactment of the fertility cycle in nature, and thus pleasing to the goddess Artemis/ Diana. This fuelled the growth of a sex trade in which people were trafficked into prostitution to satisfy the desires of 'worshippers' (typically, male) to have a 'spiritual experience' with deity. Just as he said to the churches in Rome and Corinth, Paul's point to Timothy was not about judging the *victims* of the sex trade (the prostitutes); he was demonstrating that the true God was far more knowable and without having to have sex with a temple prostitute. That's why the good news is truly good news!

It's important to acknowledge that some have questioned how prevalent prostitution was in pagan temple worship. However, the issue is not its frequency but that it happened at all and that, crucially, the Jewish Christians *believed* it was still happening.[45]

Once again, it appears there is a different way to understand what Paul was saying. He was not condemning faithful, life-long, monogamous 'until death us do part' same-sex relationships, rather the way some people are exploited and those who exploit them.

So, if the Bible's seven direct references to homosexuality don't appear to provide the clear unequivocal condemnation that some claim, what of the indirect teachings that others sometimes link as evidence of God's wrath?

To think about...

1. To what extent is sex spiritual, as well as physical and emotional?

2. Think about the lesbian, gay, bi, trans, or queer people you know. To what extent does 1 Timothy 1:10-11 accurately describe them? If not, who are these verses referring to?

9

Green and yellow specs

As a teenager I was told I needed to wear glasses. I thought, 'If I have to wear glasses, I'm going all-in'. So, I ordered a huge pair of bright green and yellow thick frames and, as if that wasn't enough, added a strong green tint to the prescription lenses. These weren't my spare pair; they were my *only* glasses which I had to wear all the time. When I wore them, people looked at me. (People can be so envious at times!) However, when I looked back at *them*, they all seemed peculiarly ill; their faces and hands looked slightly diseased or decayed. It was obviously contagious, because, when I then looked at my own hands, I too had caught whatever they had. My hands had also developed a peculiarly green tint. It was all very worrying. How I saw things was, of course, being distorted by my tinted lenses.

Bishop Lesslie Newbigin[46] said, irrespective of our need for eyewear, each of us has *invisible* lenses that filter our view of the world - in the same way that sunglasses give an altered perception of reality. These invisible lenses are based on our culture and history. They change (distort) how we see things. This led Newbigin to assert that no one is capable of reading the Bible in isolation. It's why people from different cultures and ages can have different interpretations of the same Bible passage. Just as everything seemed green when I wore my green and yellow glasses, it should come as no surprise that if we live in a sexist or homophobic society (or have been raised in a church that teaches same-sex relationships are inherently sinful), we can sometimes attach discriminatory interpretations to sections of the Bible that others wearing different cultural lenses see differently from us.[47] If not corrected, our invisible lenses play tricks with us: we either see things that are *not* there or fail to see things that *are*. Though it is not possible to remove Newbigin's invisible lenses, through a process of critical self-reflection and study, it is possible to *identify* and then *counter* their effect.

We'll explore some passages in the Bible that, whilst they don't mention same-sex relationships, are nevertheless sometimes applied as if they do. (We'll later look at passages that are not applied to same-sex attraction but probably should be.)

I've noticed some who oppose LGBTQ+ inclusion have changed their argument in recent times. They used to rely on their *direct* evidence: the seven 'clobber' verses in the Bible that *directly* reference sex between men (the ones we've explored.[48]) Their case was built on, "The Bible clearly says..." However, I believe the defence has sufficiently demonstrated these verses are instead warnings against abuse: child abuse; gang rape; male rape; sex-trafficking/ temple prostitution; slave masters abuse of power over their slaves. It would be surprising if God didn't condemn such abuses. Now, no longer able to cite these verses as credible *direct* evidence, it seems the prosecution case has now been forced to rely on *circumstantial* evidence – using verses in the Bible that make no mention of same-sex relationships as proof that God opposes same-sex relationships.

The two most cited are Genesis chapters 1-2 (Creation narratives) and Matthew chapter 19 (Jesus' answer about the validity of a specific husband and wife's divorce case). Much is made of the Bridegroom/ Bride of Christ metaphor. As we'll see, this beautifully describes Christ's relationship with His Church. That's the Church that comprises all: men and women; single/ married/ divorced/ remarried; black/ white/ brown; young/ old, straight/ gay.... This metaphor was never intended to legislate marriage between two specific individuals; if it was, single people, the bereaved, as well as those who are lesbian, gay, bi, trans or queer, and anyone else that hasn't 'tied the knot', would all be guilty of not being in a 'marriage between a man and a woman'.

To think about...

1. What are *your* 'invisible lenses'?

2. How does *your* upbringing, church belonging, or life today influence how you understand the Bible?

10

Adam & Steve?

Genesis 1-2

"Then God said, 'Let us make mankind in our image, in our likeness, so that they may rule over the fish in the sea and the birds in the sky, over the livestock and all the wild animals and over all the creatures that move along the ground.' So God created mankind in his own image, in the image of God he created them; male and female he created them. God blessed them and said to them, 'Be fruitful and increase in number; fill the earth and subdue it. Rule over the fish in the sea and the birds in the sky and over every living creature that moves on the ground.'" Genesis 1:26-28

'God created Adam and *Eve*, not Adam and *Steve*.' That's the cheap quip some use to avoid engaging with the Bible. The argument goes like this. God created a heterosexual world order based on a man and a woman. Two men or two women would have been a deviation from this plan. The inference is, this set a pattern for all men and women to subsequently follow; God's ideal being that every single male should be joined to a single woman in heterosexual marriage so that they can be 'fruitful and increase in number' (conceive and have children). This is traditionally stated at the beginning of Anglican wedding services.

There are some obvious problems with this approach. If marriage is the ideal, what does that say about those who want to be married but haven't yet met the right person? What of those who once were married but are no longer (either because of divorce or bereavement)? What does it say about the positive value of being single? And then, what of those who are married but don't have children (because they've chosen not *now* or not *ever*; are not able to have children due to fertility issues, miscarriage or stillbirth, or because they have experienced the tragedy of infant loss/ bereavement)? We must not condemn those that don't conform to a human projection of God's ideal or universal command.

Genesis was written in a pre-scientific age for a pre-scientific audience to articulate what many already instinctively knew: *we are not here by chance.* There was a time when all that we see did not exist. Then something happened. Out of nowhere (*ex nihilo*), something, someone, unbelievably powerful and yet wildly creative (the Ultimate Being - God) kicked off a sequential process that resulted in everything that we see - and are - coming into existence. The story of our 'being' is ultimately linked to, and totally dependent on, God's 'being' – our story with God's story. The whole Bible is the unfolding story of God's creation and re-creation, from alpha to omega. Genesis opens with, "*In the beginning, God* created the heavens and the earth" [1:1]

This matters because some today try to present Genesis as being a scientific and literal report of the precise mechanics God used to create the Cosmos in six 24-hour days (which just happens to be 144,000 hours – *symbolic* of total completeness[49]). What's more, some 'Young Earth'[50] advocates even believe it's all less than 10,000 years old. For them, the central point is that, on the sixth day, God created a fully developed 'man'

(Adam). Keeping with the literalism, curiously, God only later realised that something extra was needed to 'complete' the man, and so, reworked His plan, to create a 'wo-man' (Eve). They're trying to defend Genesis as 'science' when Genesis was written as a poetic narrative pointing to the bigger story of God.[51] A literal *interpretation* focuses on Adam and Eve being two literal human beings – the only two that existed initially – and that everything God said applied literally to these two individuals. However, once you become open to Genesis telling a far bigger story about all of humanity (not just about two humans), then all that God said can be shared by humanity. This is liberating. Yes, humanity procreates (collectively), but not every *individual* human must. Yes, God created men and women but that doesn't mean every man must marry a woman.

God saw all that He had made, and it was very good

The first chapter of the Bible celebrates that God did a good job with all that He made: planets, stars and moons; energy, seasons, and rhythm; plants and vegetation; animals, fish and birds. God declared it was all *good!* Then God created humans (humanity in 'Adam' and subsequently 'Eve') and declared them (us) to be *very* good [Ge.1:31]. Whilst what's become known as the doctrine of 'Original Sin'[52] focuses on the significance of chapter *three*, we do well to remember that the Bible, like all good books, starts with chapter one (not three) – what could be called, the doctrine of 'Original *Goodness*'.[53] Even after 'the Fall', God continued to refer to humanity as being made in the image of God [Ge.9:6]. That hadn't changed.

'Adam' stems from *adamah*, the ancient Hebrew for 'earth' (from which Adam was formed). In Genesis Adam refers to both a 'man' (a specific individual) [Ge.2:16] and 'mankind' (representative of all humanity – both men and women) [Ge.1:27]. Whilst Genesis 1 emphasises the commonality of humanity (men and women together), in Genesis 2's account Adam is made first. There was a time when Adam was humanity; Adam was a (the only) human, not just a man. Both his sex (male) and gender identity (maleness, what it means to be a man) only became apparent with the introduction of Eve, the 'wo-man' [Ge.2:23]'.[54] Both sex and gender are social constructs that only become visible when compared to others. God doesn't just create, He also recreates. *"In Christ, we become new creations. The old has gone, the new has come"* [2Co.5:17]. Then, our identity becomes shaped far more by our 'in Christ' status than by our gender or sexual orientation.

It is not good for the man to be alone

Relationships are at the heart of God: Father, Son and Holy Spirit co-exist together in perfect relationship as separate, co-equal persons of the Trinity. *"Then God said, 'Let us make man in our image, in our likeness..."* [Ge.1:26] Being made in the image of God, we thrive when in relationship with others. Whilst a marriage relationship might not be for everyone, co-existing with others in mutually-supportive, mutually-enriching relationships or community is.

God said everything He had made was good. Except one thing. It was *not* good for Adam to be alone. So, God created a helper. The majority identify as heterosexual, and so – if they choose – look to find their forever 'soul mate' in a member of the opposite gender. The physical and emotional intimacy they experience with their lifelong partner serves as a pattern for spiritual intimacy Christ, the Bridegroom, seeks with His Bride, the Church. Those who identify as gay find their 'soul mate' in someone of the same gender. Are we saying 'it's not good to be alone.. *unless you are gay*, in which case, you must remain alone for the duration of your whole life because the intimacy found in a lifelong partnership is only for heterosexual people'? Surely *'it is not good to be alone'* applies to all, irrespective of sexual orientation? Is God saying LGBTQ+ people are not as good as heterosexual people, and so not fit to have a 'forever partner'? Is God saying LGBTQ+ people are better than heterosexual people, and so more able to live celibately and find their intimacy with God alone?

Neither seems reasonable. Why would God want to meet some people's needs, but deliberately withhold the benefit from others? That would be to declare *good* precisely what God had originally said was *not* good![55]

I will make a helper suitable for him

Some interpret the later creation of Eve as suitable helper for Adam to mean that women must have a God-ordained *secondary*, supportive and submissive role to men, at least in a marriage relationship. This 'complementarian' thinking[56] (because, they claim, men and women have a God-ordained different but complementary role of equal value – if not equal position – to each other) must reject same-sex marriage in order to preserve the privileged rights they claim for men over women. Their patriarchal 'world order' would collapse if it turned out the 'suitable helper' for some men was another man, not a woman. For them, who would be 'head of the household'?

The Hebrew word 'ê-zer, that some translate as 'helper', is also used of God: *"The Lord is our 'ê-zer (helper) and shield."* [Ps.33:20]; *"God, you are my 'ê-zer (helper) and my deliverer."* [Ps.70:5]. Women are neither lesser nor subordinate to men, just as God isn't to humanity. They are partners, co-workers, on an equal footing. If chronology and source determine status, then men would have to be lesser to dirt. Man was incomplete and insufficient for the task of leading and caring (ministry) for all that God had made; hence why wo-man was also required to 'save Adam'. It appears God placed equity at the heart of human relationships.

Not all 'conservatives/ traditionalists' espouse a gender-hierarchy that renders women subservient to men, but many do. The same hermeneutical and cultural approach that leads them to oppose LGBTQ+ inclusion also leads them to oppose the ordination of women, not permitting them to teach or lead in the Church. They are at least consistent. Those who support the *inclusion* of women but the *exclusion* of LGBTQ+ need to ask themselves why they are inconsistent in their handling of the Scriptures (and what's behind that?)

Be fruitful and increase in number

Having blessed humanity, God said, *"Be fruitful and increase in number"* [Ge.1:28]. Under the old Covenant, the only way to grow Israel was through procreation; faith was not so much a personal choice, as a birth certificate; your inherited birth genes determined your faith (and eternal destiny.) The survival of Israel depended on couples 'being fruitful and increasing in number'. However, Christ's new Covenant heralded in a less deterministic, more inclusive, approach. Now, as Nicodemus discovered, anyone can be 'born again' into Jesus, the 'new Israel' [Jn.3:3].

Ironically, some fundamentalists appear to rely on evolutionary arguments to say the future viability of 'Project Creation' was dependent on each man procreating with a woman for the purposes of having children. They argue homosexuals, and to a lesser extent, lesbians (because they can still become pregnant), are a biological threat to the human race. For this reason, it's every man and woman's God-given duty to seek – and procreate in – a heterosexual union. Of course, many gay couples do have children (and make great parents – just as some heterosexual couples can be toxic parents) by the same means that also assist some heterosexual couples, such as donor insemination, intrauterine insemination (IUI), in vitro fertilisation (IVF), surrogacy, adoption or fostering.

There is then the rather obvious question about the grand kids – Adam and Eve's! Boy (Adam) meets girl (Eve). They had sex. Now the earth's population comprises Mum (Eve), Dad (Adam), and their three children (Cain, Abel and Seth – and possibly some daughters that no-one bothered to make note of). All very conventional. But how is God's command – "be fruitful, increase in number, fill the earth" – then to be fulfilled without incestuous sexual relations within this one family? Fundamentalists who present Genesis 1 and 2 as God's 'blueprint', setting the pattern for all future human relationships, inadvertently create a model that relies upon incest. That seems wholly unsatisfactory. If man-woman heterosexual relations are the pattern, then so too is incest. Alternatively, Genesis 1 and 2 were never intended to be as prescriptive.

The fundamentalist procreation argument appears to prioritise reproduction, rather than placing the emphasis on the fruit that comes from entering into a loving, life-long, faithful relationship (which may or may not include having children). If 'Adam' is about humanity as a whole (and, remember, initially Adam was the sum total of *all* humanity) then whilst *humanity* must reproduce, it's not the case that every single *individual* must.[57] When Adam and Eve were the sum total of humanity, the call to procreate had great urgency; now, with approaching 8 billion humans on the planet, the call to procreate seems less pressing (and even irresponsible).

Again, if God's intent was that <u>all</u> people reproduce, what of single people without a partner? What of those bereaved? What of those unable to conceive? What of those too young or too old? What of those simply wanting to delay starting a family? Are we saying that's not okay because they are *not* fulfilling God's command? Conversely, what of those who become pregnant without their consent? The result of sexual violence? The result of forced marriage[58]? Are we saying that's okay because they *are* fulfilling God's command to procreate?

Sex is not just about procreation; it's also about passion, joy, intimacy, vulnerability, and generosity. Animals 'mate' (it's their animal instinct), but two zebras aren't having that awkward conversation: are we just 'seeing each other', 'dating', or now 'exclusive'? Whilst animals are declared good, we humans are *very* good. We look more animalistic if we reduce sex to procreation or just a physical act.

That is why a man leaves his father and mother and is united to his wife, and they become one flesh

Genesis refers to being 'united' or 'joined together' with another. It makes no mention of 'marriage' *per se*. That's because 'marriage', in the sense we understand it today, is more of a social construct used to publicly recognise and bestow legal rights and responsibilities. We must not confuse our modern, Western understanding of marriage, exemplified in the Victorian-inspired 'traditional white wedding' ceremony, with marriage in the Bible. Marriage didn't become a sacrament in the Church until the twelfth century. In the Early Church couples were joined together often without formal religious ceremonies.

The act of procreation or sexual intercourse does not actually require 'leaving and cleaving', and yet from the outset, the Bible asserts the expectation of lifelong, faithful union between two people. It's not enough to simply 'go forth and multiply'; it has to be in the context of loving and faithful intimacy. That applies equally to all, irrespective of gender or sexual orientation.

Moving on, Christian understandings of the Scriptures should be Christo-centric; that is, we interpret the whole of the Scriptures through the lenses of Christ. So how did Jesus refer to Genesis?

To think about...

1. What difference does it make knowing *you* are made in the image of God? How does that help you engage with others?

2. How do you feel about others, who might be/ think totally different to you, also being made in the image of God? How does that help you engage with them?

3. Why is loneliness so bad for our health: physically, mentally, emotionally...?

11

Let's toast the Groom, Bride & the Eunuchs?

Matthew 19:1-12

"Some Pharisees came to him to test him. They asked, 'Is it lawful for a man to divorce his wife for any and every reason?' 'Haven't you read,' he replied, 'that at the beginning the Creator "made them male and female," and said, "For this reason a man will leave his father and mother and be united to his wife, and the two will become one flesh"? So they are no longer two, but one flesh. Therefore, what God has joined together, let no one separate.' 'Why then,' they asked, 'did Moses command that a man give his wife a certificate of divorce and send her away?' Jesus replied, 'Moses permitted you to divorce your wives because your hearts were hard. But it was not this way from the beginning. I tell you that anyone who divorces his wife, except* *for sexual immorality, and marries another woman commits adultery.'"* Matthew 19:3-9

In Jesus' day, marriage was the social 'norm', not the 'lifestyle option' it is today. Back then, it was rare and shocking for someone of marrying age *not* to be married. And yet Jesus Himself was not married; something His observers and critics would have been only too aware of.

The Pharisees set out to trap Jesus with, what they believed was, a no-win question about the sanctity of marriage and the right of *men* to divorce. Whilst Jesus didn't fall for it, it appears those today who oppose same-sex marriage might have. For them, the significance of Christ's response is that marriage must be – can only be – between a man and a woman.

However, the context is that Jesus was asked a *specific* question about a *specific* troubled marriage between a *specific man and a woman*. It is not surprising therefore that He approached this heterosexual scenario by talking about this *specific* man and a *woman*. In fact, Jesus answers it only from the man's/ husband's perspective, because that was the question posed: *"Jesus replied, 'Moses permitted you to divorce your wives because... (v.8) I tell you that anyone who divorces his wife, except for...'" (v.9).*

Jesus quoted from Genesis, *"For this reason a man will leave his father and mother and be united with his wife, and the two will become one flesh"* [Ge.1:27] because it was relevant Scripture to the *scenario* posed to Him. Jesus was establishing He was pro-marriage. (It's important to say, those who support same-sex marriage are also pro-marriage; that's why they want it available to all, not just some.) To say this proves marriage must always be between a man and a woman is to conflate with today's heteronormative viewpoint. It's hard to make a rule for all future pairings from a sample of just two individuals. Curiously, when it comes to *divorce*, those that oppose same-sex marriage often then become far more open to interpreting the Scriptures.

Remember, when Jesus and others in the Bible refer to 'marriage', they are mostly referring to *'arranged* marriage' (not to be confused with 'forced marriage'); they are not talking about modern Western notions of dating, romance and "she said yes" Instagram proposals. Objectors to LGBTQ+ inclusion who say they're advocating 'Biblical marriage' don't mean *that* kind of first Century *arranged* marriage, rather eighteenth or nineteenth Century patriarchal romanticism.

At a wedding, when we hear Jesus' declaration, *'What God has joined together, let no one separate'*, we know this is for the couple standing before us who have just made their vows to one another (just as it was for the specific couple Jesus was presented with.) It is not about the *institution* of marriage, as we've come to know it today. No-one is claiming that same-sex marriages took place in the Bible. But then, the Bible presents a wide variety of marital arrangements, including arranged [Ge.24], forced [De.2 2:28-29], polygamous [Ge.4:19; Jud.8:30-31; 1Ki.11:3; 1Ch.3:1-9], incest [Ge.4:16-7; 19:30-38; Ex.6:19-20; 2Ki.30:1-2], informal, highly elaborate, living together... Does the Bible *prohibit* same-sex marriage? I believe the answer to that is no. That being the case, why oppose what brings together two consenting people in a faithful, life-long, life-affirming union? Who does it harm? And especially when they seek to do so lying down together as 'a three-cord strand' [Ecc.4:11-12] – the *covenant* of marriage – the couple and God.

What is far easier to agree, Jesus was defending the validity and sanc-tity of marriage. He asserted that marriage was always intended to be monogamous: a lifelong, faithful, intimate relationship between two peo-ple. And that becoming 'one flesh' (sex) was to be an important part of this. Monogamy is not just, *don't* have sex with someone you're not married to. Monogamy as God intended is far more liberating, fulfilling and fun. It's when two people commit themselves to each other: emotionally, physical-ly, and sexually 'till death us do part'. It's two people having sex – lots of it – with each other for the rest of their married lives together. There's no need – or capacity – for sexual intimacy with anyone else because they are so focused on giving and receiving sexual intimacy with each ether. Within the safety and security of their committed relationship, they can spend a lifetime discovering what pleases each other, and how to give and receive pleasure at each successive stage of life. Even if things aren't quite right (be that for a night or a season), there is the reassurance that they are each committed to one other and their relationship to allow them time, space, and love, because neither is walking away. Marriages might suffer because of monotony but not because of authentic monogamy.

This is not about one partner asserting their right to be pleasured by the other. There's no place for demanding 'conjugal rights', as if one partner is the 'property' of the other. Paul made clear that Christ, being the ultimate Bridegroom, is the role model for all bridegrooms (husbands) to follow in the way He loves His bride, the Church. How did He love His Bride? By sacrificing Himself and His own needs for her. Again, linking back to the Genesis account, Paul asserted:

> "*Husbands, love your wives, just as Christ loved the church and gave himself up for her to make her holy, cleansing her by the washing with water through the word, and to present her to himself as a radiant church, without stain or wrinkle or any other blemish, but holy and blameless. In this same way, husbands ought to love their wives as their own bodies. He who loves his wife loves himself. After all, no one ever hated their own body, but they feed and care for their body, just as Christ does the church – for we are members of his body. 'For this reason a man will leave his father and mother and be united to his wife, and the two will become one flesh. 'This is a profound mystery – but I am talking about Christ and the church. However, each one of you*

also must love his wife as he loves himself, and the wife must respect her husband." Ephesians 5:25-35

What's more, instead of the Bride (Church) having to prove, present, or justify to the Groom (Christ) 'her' purity, the Groom (Christ) gives *His* purity to the Bride.[59] She is declared, presented, pure, not because of who she is and what she has (or has not) done, but because of who *He* is and what *He* has done. *Sola fide!* It's grace, with no asterisk, no small print. Paul developed this idea further in his letter to the Church in Corinth:

"Now for the matters you wrote about: 'It is good for a man not to have sexual relations with a woman.' But since sexual immorality is occurring, each man should have sexual relations with his own wife, and each woman with her own husband. The husband should fulfil his marital duty to his wife, and likewise the wife to her husband. The wife does not have authority over her own body but yields it to her husband. In the same way, the husband does not have authority over his own body but yields it to his wife. Do not deprive each other except perhaps by mutual consent and for a time, so that you may devote yourselves to prayer. Then come together again so that Satan will not tempt you because of your lack of self-control. I say this as a concession, not as a command. I wish that all of you were as I am. But each of you has your own gift from God; one has this gift, another has that." 1 Corinthians 7:1-7

To what extent is your church's teaching as practical and direct about sex?

So, yes, Jesus affirmed the place of marriage. But why? Because marriage is more than just a social contract between two consenting people. It is a union between two people *and God*. *"Therefore, what <u>God</u> has joined together, let no one separate"* [Mt.19:6]. Marriage between two people is also symbolic of the bigger story, the union between *Creator* and *Created*, *Christ* and *Church*, the *Bridegroom* and *Bride*. Christians who don't yet feel able to endorse same-sex relationships argue that, because Christ is the *Groom* and we, the Church, are His *Bride*, therefore human marriage can only be between a *man* and a *woman*. However, this predicates that God is *male* and *heterosexual* – both human constructs that God transcends. It also fails to recognise this as a *metaphor*. Just as John's seven *"I am.."* sayings[60] are profound metaphors that point to a bigger truth – they make no sense if taken literally (Jesus is not an actual door!) – so the Bridegroom/ Bride metaphor points to the intimate union between Christ and Church.

It is true the Bible frequently refers to God using masculine *He/ Him* pronouns. What's more, God is ascribed masculine titles such as Father and Lord. And yet no-one seriously suggests that God is *male*. After all, women, as well as men, are made in God's image [Ge.1:26-27]. As Jesus declared, 'God is spirit' [Jn.4:24], and so transcends human understandings of gender. Some might say, given the very human limitations of our understanding and language, and that those who wrote the Bible were themselves sinful people in a sinful world (who, coincidently, were all men), it is perhaps not surprising their patriarchal undertones are reflected in the text. Others will prefer to say that God graciously accommodated *Himself* to the limitations of the male authors, in order to accompany humanity on a gradual journey towards Shalom, as God always intended. Whatever, God is *not* male.

Similarly, the Church has historically been gendered *female*, and so given *she/her* pronouns. It's in the same way that ships, even trucks, have been gendered female and given 'feminine' names, presumably because those with the power to construct, control and own such 'vessels' were/are themselves men in a heteronormative, patriarchal age. Yet the Church evidently comprises women, as well as men. When Paul speaks of the Church as being the Bride of Christ, he is speaking of the total community of believers that are 'in Christ', whatever their ethnicity, socio-economic status, gender, or other human distinctions (or protected characteristics) [Gal.3:26-18]. He was not speaking of individuals. Yes, we all, as the collective Church, are the Bride of Christ. However, I as an individual, whatever my human distinctions/ characteristics, am not the Bride of Christ. To claim this metaphor proves that marriage must only be between a man and a woman, in my opinion, confuses the text. All other metaphors used in the Bible to describe the Church are inclusive of all members (army, body, building, vine/branches); the Bride metaphor is no different.

This is crucial because, in recent times, no longer able to claim the 'clobber passages' for their cause, this 'Groom and Bride' argument has become the central plank in the 'conservatives/ traditionalists' meta-narrative case. They argue the big story running through the whole of Scripture, from Genesis to Revelation, is one of redemption and the restoration of fallen humanity back into right relationship with God, Creation, and one another, brought about through the saving work of Christ. So far, so good. However, they go *'off piste'* when they start to claim that, because Christ is the Groom and the Church is the Bride, therefore every marriage between individuals can only be between a man and a woman. In doing so, I think they've tacked on to the meta-narrative additional dogma which *sounds* like Scripture, but which is in reality their own *interpretation/ application* of it. Jesus 'called out' the Pharisees for doing something similar [Mk.7:1 -13].

Similarly, Jesus rebuked the Sadducees when, in order to undermine belief in bodily resurrection, they pitched an absurd marriage scenario [Mt.22:23-33]. Their classic prequel, *One Bride for Seven Brothers*, had seven childless brothers each taking it in turns to marry their widowed sister-in-law, with each subsequently dying without a son and heir. The Sadducees wanted to know, in heaven, who would she then be married to? Jesus was clear: they'd misread both the Scriptures and God by fixating on one pixel at the expense of the bigger picture. These misogynistic Sadducees, with their talk of 'leaving a wife to his brother', like a possession bequeathed in a will, had failed to see that the Law was given, as a means of grace and justice, to protect and provide for bereaved women [De.25:5-10]. Curiously, there wasn't even a Mosaic requirement for any of the brothers to be single; the well-being of the bereaved woman mattered more than what others thought. Jesus went further: eternity with God is not dependent on whether or not our 'relationship status' in this, temporary life, is conventional or 'complicated'. Those who oppose LGBTQ+ inclusion overlook this incident!

Whilst marriage is *intended* to be "till death us do part", Jesus recognised that sometimes relationships do break down beyond repair. Many Pharisees (experts in the Law), believing God to be hard and angry towards His people, had become preoccupied with the technicalities of the law and the need to remain 'legal'; they had forgotten the Law was given to point us towards gracious and loving God – not to become a curse to us. They sought to discredit Jesus, by demonstrating He was either too lax or too judgmental about the difficult and sensitive topic of divorce.[61] As ever, Jesus' response was principally driven by love and compassion. As much as marriage is noble and good, sometimes the loving and compassionate response is to support people through their separation. In any case, Moses had been combating polygamy, whereby a *man* over a period of years might acquire multiple wives and then use frivolous reasons to divorce each (thus rendering the divorced wife poverty-stricken). Once again Jesus demonstrated that His 'yoke' (His interpretation of the Scriptures) was different to that of the Pharisees.[62] Furthermore, whilst some claim divorce is always wrong (sinful), looking at the full picture of the Bible gives a very different understanding. Again, Jesus was talking about divorce between a *man* and *woman* because that was the scenario pitched to Him by the Pharisees, not because marriage can never be between two people of the same sex. It's marriage, not the gender, which was the issue.

Those who are same-sex attracted are called to follow Christ in just the same way as everyone else. I am categorically _not_ suggesting that the Bible gives permission for people – whatever their sexual orientation – to live a lawless, hedonistic lifestyle. To become a disciple of Christ involves taking up your Cross daily to follow Him. If marriage is a gift from God that calls for faithful, lifelong commitment between two people, then the same high standards are required, whatever the sexual orientation of the couple.

> *"The disciples said to him, 'If this is the situation between a husband and wife, it is better not to marry.' Jesus replied, 'Not everyone can accept this word, but only those to whom it has been given. For there are eunuchs who were born that way, and there are eunuchs who have been made eunuchs by others – and there are those who choose to live like eunuchs for the sake of the kingdom of heaven. The one who can accept this should accept it.'"* Matthew 19:10-12

Marriage is clearly not for everyone. (Jesus Himself, along with John the Baptist and Apostle Paul, did not marry.) And now the disciples, having heard Jesus speak about the challenges of monogamous relationships, wonder whether it's better to stay celibate. Jesus goes on to say there are some people for whom a heterosexual marriage would not work.

Jesus' response surprised His disciples, and it may surprise us too. Also surprising is the lack of attention given to it by many Biblical commentators, especially Evangelical ones.[63] That's because Jesus suddenly introduced _eunuchs!_

Some say Jesus was merely advocating celibacy as an alternative to heterosexual union. Certainly, Apostle Paul would later affirm that marriage and celibacy are both gifts from God [1 Cor.7]. But what was a eunuch? And why were they relevant to what Jesus was saying about marriage?

In its most basic form, a eunuch was a male without testicles. This could have been the result of a birth defect, self-mutilation, or mutilation by others. Unable to produce hormones, eunuchs were sterile and had low or non-existent sexual function. They were viewed with suspicion and fear by some (almost mythical-like), and yet those in power found them – in a testosterone-charged culture – to be reassuringly non-threatening. Eunuchs (from the Greek 'eunoukhos', meaning 'bedroom guard') were entrusted with looking after their master's close quarters and even his harem (safe in the knowledge they would not 'make off' with his women). Some were promoted to high office, acting as their master's envoy or Chief Operating Officer, such as Potiphar[64] [Ge.39] and Daniel[65] [Dan.1].

Jesus gave three different reasons why some might be eunuchs.

First, Jesus said, *"there are eunuchs who were <u>born</u> that way"* [v.12]. This could include those born without either the sexual capability (due to a birth defect or uncorrected physical condition) or the *sexual desire* (they are simply not attracted to the opposite sex). Some opponents of equal marriage, claim same-sex attraction is a lifestyle choice that LGBTQ+ people can switch on or off (or be healed from, as if a disease). By contrast, Jesus here appeared to affirm that some are simply 'born this way'. It's not a question of environment, conditioning or culture; it's simply how they are made. They can no more choose their sexual orientation than their skin colour, height or any other biologically-determined characteristic. If it is accepted that some people are simply born gay, then surely the right response is to celebrate and declare that what God has made is indeed good. We'll look later at the profound impact of Psalm 139.

Second, Jesus says, *"there are eunuchs who have been <u>made</u> eunuchs by others"* [v.12]. Others have physically altered them. Some boys were castrated before they started puberty to ensure their bodies retained child-like features, albeit with adult-height, such as high voice, non-muscular build, small penis, and no pubic hair. These children, 'made eunuchs by others', were mutilated and then used for the sexual gratification of others. However, it's far too simplistic to claim that same-sex attraction is the result of physical or sexual abuse in childhood.

Chemical castration has been used to punish or 'treat' those convicted of homosexual acts. In 1952 Alan Turing, the British wartime code-breaking hero, was chemically castrated as an alternative punishment, having been found criminally guilty of a homosexual act. Tragically, two years later he killed himself. It was not until 2013 that the British Government initiated a Royal Pardon. Many others less famous than Turing have not received similar apologies. Today in some parts of the world LGBTQ+ people continue to be treated as criminals, made eunuchs by forced chemical castration.

Third, Jesus said, *"there are those who <u>choose</u> to live like eunuchs for the sake of the kingdom of heaven"* (v.12). This is often used to justify those that have taken a vow of celibacy as part of their 'holy orders'. To devote themselves wholeheartedly to the service of God and others, they opt not to be distracted by a marriage relationship. They live *like* eunuchs because they have not actually been physically castrated. It's rather that they either have a low sexual drive or choose to live a life that is not determined by their sexual drive.

Today, some same-sex attracted Christians believe *(or have been told)*, for God's sake, they must live a celibate life. Whilst they accept they are same-sex attracted, they believe *(or have been told)* it would be sinful for them to have a monogamous sexual relationship with someone of the same sex. They therefore live in denial of their sexuality out of their devotion to God - for the sake of the Kingdom of Heaven. People must be allowed to make their own responses. However, it would be tragic if some make such a sacrifice due more to misinformation than personal conviction. Celibacy is for some (be they heterosexual or homosexual), but it is not the only option for Christians who are same-sex attracted.

Judaism didn't support genital castration. The Law stated, *"No one who has been emasculated by crushing or cutting may enter the assembly of the Lord"* [Dt.23:1]. Eunuchs were not allowed to become priests or enter the tabernacle. They were outsiders simply because of their lack of testicles.

Jesus chose to go against the religious flow and affirm eunuchs. As well as showing His understanding (including His awareness that they weren't simply 'all the same'), Jesus affirmed their faith. Whilst Jesus was referring to eunuchs, not LGBTQ+ people we know today, there is nevertheless good parallel with the way Jesus chose to respond to eunuchs and how we should affirm those today who are queer.

To think about...

1. Should Christian sexual ethics apply differently or the same to 'straight' and gay people?

2. Is divorce ever permissible? How should the Church respond to those who are divorced?

3. How has society and Church used violence, be that physical, psychological or spiritual, to 'correct' queer people of their sexual orientation? What has been the impact on them?

12

Yes, but Sodom & Gomorrah...
Jude 5-7

"Though you already know all this, I want to remind you that the Lord at one time delivered his people out of Egypt, but later destroyed those who did not believe. And the angels who did not keep their positions of authority but abandoned their proper dwelling – these he has kept in darkness, bound with everlasting chains for judgment on the great Day. In a similar way, Sodom and Gomorrah and the surrounding towns gave themselves up to sexual immorality and perversion. They serve as an example of those who suffer the punishment of eternal fire."

Jude 5-7

J ude and his friends were challenged to contend for the faith, resisting the subtle abuse of grace by those who brought division through their unrestrained lawlessness. It appears some had mistakenly thought grace meant they could do whatever they liked, without any consequences or reference to God. These godless men had changed the grace of God into a licence for immorality, and were following their natural instincts, perversions, and evil desires. Jude was reminded of what had happened to Sodom and Gomorrah and the surrounding towns. It appears a similar culture had developed in Jude's time and place.[66]

Remember, the sin exposed in Sodom and Gomorrah was not that of a couple entering into a faithful, 'till death us do part', same-sex relationship – but rape; men raping men, male gang rape. So, yes, those who use sexual violence to brutalise, dehumanise and humiliate others are to be considered godless and immoral people who have given themselves over to their base instincts, perversions and evil desires. No wonder that God condemns such actions. So should we. It would seem disingenuous to apply this to monogamous, faithful same-sex relationships. Trace all references to Sodom and Gomorrah through the Bible, and none of them identifies sexual orientation as a factor. Only Jude links it to sex, but that turns out to be sexual violence (rape, male rape, male gang rape.) All other references are, for example, to idolatry [De.29:23], exploitation of the poor [Isa.3:9; Am.4:11], arrogance and pride [Isa.13:19].

> *"Now **THIS** was the sin of your sister Sodom: she and her daughters were arrogant, overfed and unconcerned; they did not help the poor and needy.* [50] *They were haughty and did detestable things before me. Therefore I did away with them as you have seen."*
> Ezekiel 16:49-50

The Living Bible imposes its own application when it translates 'sarkos heteras' [v.7] as 'lust of men for other men'. Others use 'perversion' (Good News, NIV), 'unnatural relations' (RSV) or, better still, 'strange flesh' (King James Version). It literally means 'other flesh'. Noting that Lot's two visitors were angels, and that Jude already cites 1 Enoch [Jude 14-15], Jonathan Tallon, in his excellent book *Affirmative*[67], says the warning is for angels and humans (being 'other flesh' to each other) to refrain from having sex with one another. I might add, as humans are to refrain from having sex with animals (equally 'other flesh'). Again, in Sodom and Gomorrah men didn't just want sex with angels, they were attempting to *rape* them.

It's amazing how Sodom and Gomorrah keeps being brought up, even when it's known to be a judgement against sexual violence and gang rape, not a comment on consensual, committed, faithful, same-sex relationships. It seems hearsay and poor Biblical literacy is hard to shake off.

By contrast, Jude was reminded to remain in God's love and show mercy to others.

To think about...

1. Why can it be so hard to 'shake off' some inherited assumptions/ past teachings?

2. Does sexual freedom have boundaries? What are yours? Over time, have they changed? How? Why?

13

Celibacy?

1 Corinthians 7:1-40

"Now for the matters you wrote about: 'It is good for a man not to have sexual relations with a woman.'² But since sexual immorality is occurring, each man should have sexual relations with his own wife, and each woman with her own husband." 1 Corinthians 7:1-2

Some in the Church at Corinth were telling Paul, *"It is good for a man not to have sexual relations with a woman."*[v.1] (though not, as earlier editions of the NIV mistranslated, 'not to marry'.[68])

Paul didn't agree.

Faced with a highly sexualised, promiscuous culture in which 'anything goes', including Temple prostitution and abuse, some in the Church were advocating that people, whether married or single, should abstain from sex altogether. They viewed it as carnal indulgence of the 'flesh' – sinful. Yet, like many abstinence movements, it appears the prohibition was leading to guilt and duplicitous 'secret sex'. Paul's advice was surprising: have *more*, not less, sex; best expressed in faithful, monogamous, committed relationships.

In Roman culture, marriage was more a living arrangement than a legal ceremony.[69] Much emphasis was placed on the perceived social status of the household – being seen to be doing well, living well. In this male-centric Roman world, where women were rendered subservient, Paul radically challenged the gender *status quo*: husbands were to give themselves physically (sexually) to their wives, as much as wives to their husbands. This was a call for 'equal marriage' that was just as radical *then* as the call for 'equal marriage', as understood *today*, is. Sex was for women, as well as for men – mutual satisfaction. Good sex helps strengthen a committed relationship, reducing the risk of unfaithfulness [v.5] or 'paid sex' [1Co.6:15-16].

Paul conceded, if – and only if – both partners agree, then, as a spiritual discipline, during a season of prayer, they could 'fast' from sex; but only for a limited time before coming back together sexually [v.5]. Could this be the key to boosting participation in our weeks of prayer? Just imagine! For Paul, this was a concession, not a command [v.6]. With great humility, Paul twice made clear he was expressing his own *personal opinion*, not necessarily that of God's. In verse 12 he said, *"I say this (I, not the Lord)"*. In verse 25 he was even clearer: *"I don't have a command from the Lord about people who have never been married [or never had sex] but I'll give you my opinion as someone you can trust because of the Lord's mercy."* Yet, in verse 10, he was confident to say, *"I give this command (not I, but the Lord)"*. It's tempting to presume what we say, even what Apostle Paul says, is "thus saith the Lord", when it may be anything but.

Paul was openly not married. He did not have a wife to appear loyally at his side in a ministry photo or church leadership gallery.[70] In a heteronormative world, where marriage was the 'norm', this would have raised eyebrows, probably even suspicion. Whilst Paul was comfortable with who he was (no suggestion that he was gay, at least not from me, though some have wondered[71]), and wished others could experience the same, he nevertheless was gracious and pragmatic enough to recognise, what was right for him, was not necessarily right for everyone. How refreshing, especially when you consider today some who oppose LGBTQ+ inclusion demand that everyone else be and think as they.

Compared to those advocating a 'conservative' and restricting approach to sex, Paul could easily have been labelled a revisionist liberal. He applied the teaching that Jesus gave in a *Jewish* context about divorce in ways slightly different for his *Gentile* mission. Paul recognised a plurality of relational set-ups: an *indicative*, not exhaustive, drop-down menu. He addressed those who are married and those who are single; those once married but now widowed, and those who wish they had never got married in the first place; those in mixed relationships, with partners from other religions, and those who have never had sex. Not bad for one chapter.

To all, his approach was pragmatic. Being in a relationship can be a God-gift; choosing not to be in a relationship can equally be a God-gift [v.7]. Whatever your 'relationship status', we are all sexual beings; if you find yourself full of sexual passion (πυροῦσθαι / purousthai – set on fire with desire), don't succumb to transactional sex. Instead, you are free to enjoy sex in a committed, mutual-giving relationship [1Co.7:7-9]. This must surely apply to all, whatever one's sexuality. It would seem unfair to give 'straight' people this outlet, whilst requiring those who are queer to burn-up with unexpressed and repressed desires that, they are told, must never be fulfilled in their lifetime. It is surely unfair to judge LGBTQ+ people for having 'sex outside of marriage', whilst prohibiting them the opportunity to marry.

Paul had a rule for his churches: *"Each person should live as a believer in whatever situation the Lord has assigned to them, just as God has called them"* [v.17]. If they were born Jewish, then, on later becoming part of the church, they shouldn't be required to change what they were born with – a phallic symbol of identity – and pray back a foreskin! [v.18] We might similarly say, people should be affirmed 'in whatever situation the Lord has assigned them, just as God has called them', whether lesbian, gay, bi, trans, or queer. Circumcised or uncircumcised, straight or gay: what matters is keeping God's commands.

Then, in verses 21-24, Paul sets a hermeneutical challenge for those who object to, so called, revisionist interpretations of Scripture. He appears to accept the barbaric and de-humanising practice of slavery, even telling slaves, *"Don't let it trouble you"* [v.21]. Fortunately, many 'conservative/traditionalist' commentators do a commendable job in countering this misinterpretation, demonstrating that, dig deeper, and both Paul and the 'arc of Scripture' point to the rightful condemnation of the slave trade. Why can't the same hermeneutical principles be applied to the emancipation of LGBTQ+ people?

Paul doesn't address same-sex couples because, first, the *specific* statement posed to him was about a man and woman; so that's the question he answered. Second, Paul was addressing a heteronormative world that just assumed marriage (however that was formalised) could only be between a man and woman. First century understandings of sexual orientation were nothing like what we know today.

To think about...

1. Whatever your 'relationship status' or sexual orientation, what does it mean for *you* to be a sexual being?

2. How do you explain the references to slaves and slavery? Do you apply the same or different principles to explain references to sexuality? Why?

3. Is celibacy a gift for some or a requirement for all? What about for those who are LGBTQ+? Why?

14

Black and gay?

Acts 8:26-40

"As they travelled along the road, they came to some water and the eunuch said, 'Look, here is water. What can stand in the way of my being baptised?' And he gave orders to stop the chariot. Then both Philip and the eunuch went down into the water and Philip baptised him. When they came up out of the water, the Spirit of the Lord suddenly took Philip away, and the eunuch did not see him again, but went on his way rejoicing."
Acts 8:36-39

In the Book of Acts, Deacon Philip had a profound encounter with an Ethiopian eunuch who was spiritually open to exploring faith. Considering Christ's references to eunuchs, read again Acts 8:26-40.

Things had got tense for the first Christians. Pharisee Saul and the religious elite were persecuting the Christ-followers, and Stephen had just been stoned to death. No longer safe in Jerusalem, the Believers scattered far and wide. Philip went north into Samaria, where he soon found himself in the middle of revival. Amazing things were happening, huge numbers were turning to Christ. Only recently, he'd been 'waiting on tables'. Now look at him! But then God interrupted Philip's flow. Whilst it was good so many from the Jerusalem region were discovering Christ, God had a much bigger plan. God wanted (and still does want) ALL people to know him, not just those nearby, who look like, sound like, identify like, us. So, God directed Philip to double-back south, out of Samaria, back through Jerusalem, and down towards Egypt *and beyond*.

To think about...

1. It was no accident that Philip encountered the eunuch. God was behind it, Philip was willing, and the eunuch was open. What might this suggest for you and your church's mission and ministry with LGBTQ+ people today?

2. *'What can stand in the way of my baptism?'* said the eunuch. How would you answer that question if it was asked by a queer person in your church today?

3. The encounter with Philip left the eunuch *rejoicing*. To what extent does your church foster the same response from LGBTQ+ people today?

4. The new convert does not appear to have been told to change his eunuch status/ orientation. What does your church expect of new believers?

Whilst on route, possibly in modern-day Sudan, East Africa[72], Philip saw an elaborate chariot, probably with outriders. Whether just curious or nudged by God, he started a conversation. The Eunuch (we don't know his name, no one thought to record it) was clearly an 'insider', a person with power and prestige in Ethiopia. Did meeting Philip leave him feeling an 'outsider', becoming more aware of his blackness, his different religion, and his eunuch status? Male, white heteronormative cultures very quickly render people as "other". It's a powerful form of judgement and social control.

This then becomes a story of intersectionality, where multiple social-political individual characteristics, such as age, disability, gender reassignment, marriage and civil partnership, pregnancy and maternity, race, religion or belief, sex, and sexual orientation, *intersect* and often overlap, for one individual or group. In male, white, heteronormative UK it is hard to be female when sexism and misogyny (direct, indirect, and institutional) are still so evident; similarly, it can be hard to be a person of colour when racism (direct, indirect, and institutional) is also still so evident; and, of course, it can be hard to be 'out' as lesbian, gay, bi or trans when homophobia and transphobia (direct, indirect, and institutional) are still alive and kicking. Each form of oppression is wielded by the all-powerful 'normative' majority (who decide what is 'normal'), each with its own history, outrages and levels of injustice and inhumanity. To experience just one form of oppression is so hard and unjust. Privilege attempts to down-play the experience of oppression by treating each source in isolation. Intersectionality, on the other hand, recognises, that, for example, to be black, female *and* queer is to experience *multiple* and *cumulative* oppressions in one human frame. Stopped by Philip, the Ethiopian Eunuch is suddenly all too aware of intersectionality (if not yet the terminology); he is black, from an African nation, with a different religion, and is a 'eunuch'.

Many within our churches not only experience oppression in their workplaces, neighbourhoods, on a night out, or in their families, they come to church – the one place that's meant to be different – and they experience it again. What happens when your oppressor is also your church?[73] When the people who are called to model 'Heaven on earth', instead seem more content with their fiery judgments that feel more like torment from 'the other place'? Of course, many more are simply passive (though, in doing so, they collude with oppression.)

I am privileged in so, so many ways. I'm cis, male, white, middle class, privately-educated, heterosexual, neuro-typical (as far as I know), and able-bodied. I tick all the boxes. It has taken me decades to understand what *privilege* is and does, even longer to accept that I am where I am in life only *because* of my privilege, and longer still to learn and then seek to change my approach towards others. I am a privileged work-in-progress. I'm only now just beginning to see that the many challenges made over the years to my privilege (as uncomfortable as they have made me feel), have been a gracious and compassionate gift, for which I am increasingly grateful. I know full well I have represented, and too often to my shame been, the oppressor. With multiple privileges, I have not experienced the oppression that others have. How did I not see this before?

Intersectionality recognises that oppression does not operate in silos. Individuals who have experienced one form of oppression, can find solidarity with those whose oppression is different from their own. This was beautifully illustrated in the film, Pride[74], which told the story of how a group of lesbian, gay, bi and trans people, who had experienced much oppression simply because of their sexuality, stood in solidarity with the National Union of Miners in their fight for jobs and their way of life in mining communities. It is hard to imagine two more distinct groups: 'gays' and 'miners'. And yet they eventually became united in their solidarity with one another: their own experience of oppression helped them see, and stand with, those who also experienced oppression – albeit different from their own. To stand in solidarity with one another, miners didn't have to 'come out', LGBTQ+ people didn't have to 'dig down' underground.

The Ethiopian Eunuch reminds us that LGBTQ+ people are not all white. They are also black, and brown, have heritage from Brazil, India, Iran, Jamaica, Nigeria, Sudan, as well as Britain, USA... There are currently 63 countries around the world that still *criminalise* homosexuality, including Afghanistan, Ghana, Jamaica, Kenya, Nigeria, and Uganda.[75]

Some even impose the death penalty. More tragic than ironic, the British Empire exported its poisonous prejudice across its 'pink world', leaving behind oppressive colonial systems that continue today to oppress LGBTQ+ people. Intersectionality calls for LGBTQ+ communities to stand in solidarity with those whose experience of oppression today is the legacy of colonialism. You don't have to be black to take a stand as an ally against racism and oppressive imperialism. Equally, you don't have to be gay to take a stand as an ally against homophobia.

If it's too soon to identify the 'elephant in the room', or not the place of someone as privileged as I to do so, please call me out! Intersectionality challenges *all* people, including people of colour, to stand in solidarity with LGBTQ+ communities. Fortunately, there are great people (in my church and elsewhere) plus organisations doing just this. For example, Rev'd Jide Macaulay, British-Nigerian founder and CEO of House of Rainbow[76] and Revd Jarel Robinson-Brown, a British-born Jamaican Anglican Priest. It's important to acknowledge the courage that is required to do this, not just in white-majority churches, but also in black majority churches. As leading Black theologian Professor Anthony Reddie acknowledges, *"some Black people have spoken of 'paying the price' for seeking to speak 'truth to church power', when challenging issues of patriarchy and homophobia in the Church."*[77] Professor Robert Beckford puts it, *"Many Black people and the churches they attend are reasonably content to invoke a Black Christ if He is being used to attack racism. But once the question moves to sexism, and particularly the affirmation of gay, lesbian, bi-sexual and transgendered people, then the acceptability of the Black Christ dissipates markedly."*[78] I've had some ministers of colour – leaders within large black-majority churches and denominations – tell me they are sympathetic to my 'affirming' stance on LGBTQ+ justice, but that their churches would never tolerate it, so they stay silent. I understand the pressure they are under, and the need to utilise energy for the very real and ongoing fight against racism, but wonder if the righteous struggle against racism will be shortened or elongated by the tolerance of homophobia? As Dr Martin Luther King declared, *"Injustice anywhere is a threat to justice everywhere."*

Back to the text! Evidently, God was already at work in this person's life. Somehow, he'd stumbled across Isaiah:

> **"He was led like a sheep to the slaughter, and as a lamb before its shearer is silent, so he did not open his mouth. In his humiliation he was deprived of justice. Who can speak of his descendants? For his life was taken from the earth."** Isaiah 53:7

Though he didn't understand what it was about, he too was curious, and it seemed significant. Just at that moment, Philip turned up. It's one of those coincidences, 'chance encounters' that change us. God nudged Philip: don't wait for the right opening, create one. Go up to him, overcome your social awkwardness and engage this stranger in conversation. Be curious, cross both the street and cultural divide. As a result, the Gospel spread to Africa, not by "white missionaries" exporting religion and colonialism, but through an African-led movement. It was truly *Kingdom, not Empire!*

But there's still that eunuch thing. Now, it's our turn to be curious. Those that stop to ask, are often satisfied to think a eunuch was a civic ruler – like a Chancellor of the Exchequer. As we've seen from Matthew 19, it was a bit more than that: a eunuch was a man with no testicles.

Whatever, eunuchs stood out as different. They were viewed with suspicion and fear by some (almost mythical-like.)

There was something about their identity, sexual identity, that was distinct. Judaism didn't support genital castration. Consequently, eunuchs were prevented from becoming priests or entering the tabernacle. And yet this man had made the long trip from Ethiopia to Israel to check out Yahweh and to worship [v.27]. On arrival, was he welcomed? Was it a genuine 'no small print'/ 'no conditions apply' welcome, or was it the *limited welcome* that many LGBTQ+ people experience that claims to be welcoming, and yet soon reveals a toxic homophobic ethos and culture? For his own safety and mental well-being, did he keep quiet about his identity? Did what he wore give him a way? Did he learn to 'tone it down' in the Temple?

Through this experience, Philip understood God doesn't just love everyone, God loves <u>EVERYONE;</u> whatever their sexual identity – those with testicles, those without testicles, and those transitioning.

But the story doesn't end with a nice 'everyone is special' message – a shareable meme. Experiencing that God-directed/ Philip-ministered affirmation, led to change. Not: if you want to be 'one of us', in our religious crowd, you need to change your identity, stop being a eunuch – *sow 'em back on!* It was way more authentic than that: enough to convince this person to go all-in for God. If that is what God is like, count me in. Repent (change your direction) *and be baptised.*

"Here is water. What can stand in the way of me being baptised?" [Ac.8:36], asked the Eunuch. How many churches have denied baptism (or Communion, membership...) to those they've labelled different or 'sinners'? Tragically, far too many lesbian, gay, bi, and trans people haven't been left rejoicing by their encounters with Christians. It's left them feeling judged, excluded. "othered". No wonder so many have rejected God. Some of those that do pursue God are forming their own churches where they are safe and affirmed as God has wired them to be. Just in the same way that 60-70 years ago many of those who migrated to the UK received such appalling, discriminatory treatment from churches – sometimes explicit, more often subtle.

Our call and profound privilege is to be more Philip in our affirmation.

To think about...

1. What does privilege look like for you? In what ways are you privileged?

2. How has your inherited culture/ ethnicity/ upbringing shaped your attitudes towards/ beliefs about those who are queer?

3. To what extent are you an *ally* of LGBTQ+ people? How are you demonstrating this?

15

With discretion

Luke 7:1-10

"Jesus entered Capernaum. There a centurion's ser-vant, whom his master valued highly, was ill and about to die. The centurion heard of Jesus and sent some el-ders of the Jews to him, asking him to come and heal his servant. When they came to Jesus, they pleaded earnestly with him, 'This man deserves to have you do this, because he loves our nation and has built our synagogue.' So Jesus went with them." Luke 7:1-6

I believe every word that Jesus is recorded as saying about sexuality and orientation. Jesus said.. *nothing!* Given how much is said today by those who seek to condemn same-sex relationships and equal marriage, it's worth remembering that Jesus Himself, said nothing about it.

Some who don't yet feel able to support LGBTQ+ inclusion, like Wheaton College's Stanton Jones, accept "Jesus did not speak explicitly to homosexual conduct"; yet claim, "neither did He speak of rape, incest or sex with animals."[79] To equate being gay with rape is profoundly offensive, and reveals the depth of prejudice that *some* react from.

Others argue Jesus' silence was because same-sex attraction was not a Jewish issue. Had it been, they say, He would have addressed it (and, they *presume*, condemned it). But that seems a little naïve. We know that homosexuality was a feature of Roman life and that, by the time of Jesus' public ministry, the Romans had occupied Israel for almost a hundred years. Does this 'back story' explain Jesus' encounter with the Roman Centurion [Mt.8; Lk.7]?

The Centurion, despite being the local commander and therefore representative of the military oppressors, had earnt the respect of many local people because of his 'hearts and minds' support for the Jewish community. He was taking a *huge* personal risk by asking help for his sick slave from local religious people. As a Centurion, he was supposed to enforce 'Caesar is Lord'.[80] But he was desperate, so much, he asked Jewish elders to find 'this Jesus' who was said to have healing powers.

But *why* the desperation?

Dr Luke recorded, *"a Centurion's servant, whom his master valued highly, was ill and about to die"* [Lk.7:2]. This Centurion had a special attachment to one particular servant and so, when he became critically ill, the Centurion 'threw caution to the wind' in search of a cure.

He found it in Jesus.

Incidentally, many Bible translators today prefer 'servant' to the more accurate 'slave'. This is a story about a Centurion who had *slaves*. Many modern translators have adjusted the linguistics to fit our age which, rightly, rejects slavery (just as we saw they've done with *'malakoi'* and *'arsenokoítēs'* [*1Co.6:9*].) Whilst there *was* a time when the Bible (including this incident with the Centurion) was used to justify slavery as part of God's ordained structure for humanity, the translators rightly recognise the trajectory of the Bible rejects slavery, so they substitute 'servant' for 'slave'. Translators need to show the same courage when dealing with the texts associated with same-sex attraction?

So, why get emotional over what, for a Roman, was merely an asset, like a workhorse or today's vacuum cleaner, not a person?

It was not uncommon in Roman culture for some male slaves to provide a sexual function for their masters. For a Centurion posted for long periods far from home, having such a slave would have provided some relief.

Luke employs some ambiguity, first using the more common δοῦλος doulos/ slave [v.2], but then the rarer παῖς pais/ young slave [v.7]. Matthew and Luke do *not* provide enough information for us to say with certainty the Roman Centurion had a sexual involvement with his young male slave (at least not in the way sexual orientation is understood today). But, given what we know of Roman culture, neither can it be ruled out. If the Centurion was same-sex attracted, Jesus' response would be all the more remarkable and poignant for today. Far from condemning this 'outsider', Jesus commended the Centurion's faith and healed his servant. What's more, if Jesus opposed homosexuality, this situation would have given Him ample opportunity to have said so – but He didn't.

What is beyond question is just how radically inclusive Jesus was. Luke demonstrates how Jesus frequently broke religious and social conventions of His day to *include* those that others *excluded*. Women, children, the sick, 'sinners', all found life-changing acceptance. The list was *indicative* not exhaustive. The message was that Jesus overcomes social, religious, and cultural barriers to include people. To be a follower of Christ today is to be as inclusive in our dealings with people – all people, as Christ was.

> ### To think about...
> 1. When do you feel an 'outsider'? What does that do to you?
>
> 2. Why is it still difficult in traditionally male-dominated occu-pations (military, police, construction?) to be out as queer?
>
> 3. Why is 'toxic masculinity' so toxic?

16

When theology catches up

Acts 10-11

"Peter saw heaven opened and something like a large sheet being let down to earth by its four corners. It contained all kinds of four-footed animals, as well as reptiles and birds. Then a voice told him, 'Get up, Peter. Kill and eat.' 'Surely not, Lord!' Peter replied. 'I have never eaten anything impure or unclean.' The voice spoke to him a second time, 'Do not call anything impure that God has made clean.'" *Acts 10:11-15*

The Book of Acts charts the transformation from a small, exclusive sect of Christ-followers within Judaism, located in an outpost at the far end of the Roman Empire, into the worldwide universal movement that we call Christianity. It began as only applying to, and being accessible for, those of Jewish heritage. Acts chapters 10 and 11, and again in 15, are key to seeing how 'the rest of us' Gentiles (those not born Jewish) came to be radically included. Whilst these chapters do not refer to sexuality, they nevertheless provide a powerful and necessary reminder to us that, unlike dogma, the unchanging, God-breathed Word of God is living and active [Heb.4:12]. But, reader be warned: the Word of God is sharper than any doubled-edged sword, it penetrates to dividing even soul and spirit, joints and marrow; it judges the thoughts and attitudes of the heart. It doesn't just judge *"others"* (especially those we think warrant it); it judges *us* too.

As a Roman centurion, Cornelius was an agent of imperialist oppression. He was one of the invaders that the Zealots were in armed struggle against. Not only did the Roman army defeat and brutally suppress the local population, it defiled the land with its cult of 'Caesar as Lord'. Cornelius was everything the Hebrews opposed; ironic, given that he was intrigued by this Yahweh and dubbed a 'God-fearer'.

If you've ever felt an 'outsider', so did Cornelius. He was a 'not'. He was *not* in a prestigious Roman Legion but the lesser Italian Regiment (which Josephus, the Jewish-Roman historian, says was formed of Syrian auxiliaries.) This meant he was *not* a Roman citizen. Though he now had some belief in God, he was *not* a Christ-follower or a circumcised Jew. As well as the isolation that goes with rank, he was under suspicion: by the Roman empire, for his collusion with the local population he was meant to be controlling; by the Jewish diaspora, suspicious of his motives and the dilution of their Hebraic ethnicity-based community; by the Christ-followers, worried it was all a trap – after all, hadn't the Romans crucified Christ? Though not accepted by the religious, he was accepted by God.

Then, one day at three in the afternoon[81] (get ready for lots of threes, it is Peter after all), Cornelius had a vision of an angel who called him by name (most others addressed him by rank.) Whilst the 'insiders' were at the Temple in Jerusalem doing their religious duty, this 'outsider' – not welcome in the Temple – was having a profound encounter with God. Though an agent of 'Caesar is Lord', he deferred, 'What is it, *Lord?*' [v.3-4]

God said, *"send for Simon, nicknamed Peter. He's staying with Simon the tanner"* [v.5-6]. Tanners were judged 'unclean', even 'sinners', because of their contact with dead animals, blood, and faeces [Lev.11:26-28]. Was this tanner also colluding with Empire by making belts, boots, and braces for the Roman occupiers? Jews knew not to become 'contaminated by association'. In accepting hospitality from this tanner, Simon Peter probably thought he was being inclusive (he was), yet he was about to be stretched to inclusion *and beyond*. He had spent three years seeing glimpses of God's Kingdom, heaven on earth, as Jesus went *'and beyond'*, radically including, healing, restoring those on the margins. Then, on the Day of Pentecost, Peter had experienced the Spirit of Christ impacting those *'and beyond'* Jerusalem. This Gospel was for all, not just the 'usual suspects'. So, yes, Peter was signalling God's inclusivity by staying with Simon the tanner. But even those who *think* they are inclusive sometimes need reminding that God is more inclusive than His followers. Many of those who oppose LGBTQ+ inclusion are inclusive in many other ways. Acts 11 is a reminder to check for 'blind spots'.

Just as Cornelius' troops arrived to collect him, Peter was praying. Maybe, because he was hungry, his mind wandered off. (Were the hanging carcasses making him think of food?) Whatever, Peter had a vision: heaven opened, and a huge sheet (a tablecloth?) was lowered by its four corners to earth; it contained all sorts of four-footed animals, reptiles, and birds. And a voice from heaven said, *"Get up, Peter. Kill and eat!"* [v.13]

Born Jewish and living all his life according to the strict food laws specified in Leviticus 11, Peter would have been utterly repulsed at the idea of eating such unclean foods. (Like I am of eating a wiggity grub or a cute guinea pig.) He said as much. It went against everything he had been taught, it was contrary to the 'traditional view' and, as far as he was concerned it went against Scripture. No, he would not *Catch it. Kill it. Eat it.* Do we experience the same reflex revulsion when challenged by things that appear outside of our experience or inherited religious or cultural framework? Just as it was hard for Peter, so it can be for us to reappraise long-held attitudes towards LGBTQ+ inclusion, separating out Biblical interpretation from our inherited cultural or religious prejudice. No wonder Peter was 'greatly puzzled'. Maybe you are too. Having believed same-sex relationships are wrong, maybe you find yourself now 'greatly puzzled' by your gradual warming to a more inclusive stance?

Yes, *some* of the animals in the sheet would have been 'clean' (lawful to eat), but how to separate them and, in any case, wouldn't the 'unclean' (unlawful to eat) creatures have contaminated those that were deemed acceptable, rendering them also unclean by association? How often have holiness movements descended into closed separatist fortresses to avoid 'contamination with the world'? Ironic, given that the source of all holiness, Jesus Christ, spent so much time on the margins with those the 'religious elite' labelled unclean. Peter was realising, true cleanliness was not dependent on birth (nature) or behaviour (nurture), rather on the saving work of Christ. I am clean, not because of who I am or what I do or say, but because of Christ: who He is and what Christ has done and says [2Co.5:17; Tit.3:3-7].

Yes, as far as Peter understood, these foods were strictly unlawful, against the will of God. But the voice from Heaven came back, *"Do not call anything impure that God has made clean"* [Ac.10:15]. It's clear this was being applied to people (anyone), not just of animals (anything). To underline this, Peter had to hear this *three* times. Some of us need to hear the call to inclusion *and beyond* many more times before recognising and renouncing our prejudices.

Read this again a number of times, and slowly; each time placing the emphasis on a different word. Linger with this:

> **"Do not call anything impure that God has made clean."**   *Acts 10:15*

And then the doorbell went, and Cornelius' detachment of three soldiers were outside to take him to the Roman garrison at Caesarea. Peter's head must have been spinning. He wouldn't go alone, he'd take witnesses (three? No, six! Okay, two threes) Even though God said to go immediately, so ingrained was it within him, first Peter felt obligated to practise the hospitality code: he invited the three, who represented everything Peter was against or feared, to stay for the rest of the day and night... eat at his table, sleep in his beds! Was Peter already beginning to sense how God was nudging him?

The next day, having spent a further day and overnight travelling with the three, on arrival at three in the afternoon at Cornelius' substantial property, Peter quickly made the connection: *this* (clean/unclean *foods*) is really about *that* (clean/ unclean *people*). But Peter was on the backfoot. It appears Cornelius anticipated Peter was bringing a message from God; he'd assembled his family, associates, key staff to hear it [v.24]. Just as God had told Cornelius but not yet Peter, so it appears wider society has been quicker than the Church to embrace God's inclusion *and beyond*.

Spending time with Cornelius, asking questions, and listening to the stories of those with 'lived experience' [v.29-30] enabled Peter to work through his social and religious objections. Then, with great humility, Peter became convinced: *"God has shown me that I should not call any one impure or unclean* [v.28]. He probably thought he already was inclusive (don't we all?), but God was stretching him (and us) to inclusion *and beyond*. *"I now realise how true it is that God does not show favouritism but accepts everyone from every nation who fear Him and do what is right."* [Ac.10:34-35]. This humility is for us all, whether 'liberal', 'progressive' or 'conservative/ traditionalist'.

Some who oppose LGBTQ+ inclusion say God's acceptance of 'everyone from every nation' only applies to those who 'fear Him *and do what is right.*' Yet, surely the point was, God is emphatically not taking us back to the Levitical code of Leviticus 11:1-47 & 20:24-26. Instead, we are to understand the whole of Scripture, including Leviticus, through the revelation of Christ. Hadn't Jesus declared all foods clean? [Mk.7:19] Just as the Angel had told unclean 'outsider' shepherds about the birth of Jesus, *"Do not be afraid. I bring you good news of great joy that will be for all* _people… A Saviour has been born <u>to you</u>"_ [Lk.2:10-11], so Gentile Cornelius was to be one of those upon whom God's favour rests.[82]

Whilst Peter was in full flow, the Holy Spirit came on all who heard the message [v.44]. Just as had happened on the Day of Pentecost, so people – this time, _Gentile_ people – began to speak in tongues and praise God [v.46]. What could prevent them from being baptised? Dogma, tradition, intransigence, prejudice, yes; but _not_ God! Why? Peter says they have received the Holy Spirit _just as we have_. They are no longer "other"; in Christ, they are "us". This is a story of two conversions: Cornelius was converted to a new awareness of Christ, but Peter was also converted to inclusion _and beyond_. It ended with Peter demonstrating God's acceptance of Cornelius by accepting his offer of hospitality (which would previously have been unlawful for a Jew like Peter due to compromise of food and other Levitical laws.)

Word soon spread about Peter's deviation from tradition and failure to uphold the Law. This required a meeting of Council/ Synod. Perhaps not surprisingly, there Peter was heavily criticised by the 'conservative' believers. Sadly, their initial objection was not that Gentiles had received the word of God, it was that Peter had had fellowship with them [Ac.11:1-3]. Peter explained in detail the circumstances that had led him to take this radical inclusion approach. He had been led by the Holy Spirit and, it transpires, this had always been God's intent. _"Who was I to think that I could oppose God?"_ [Ac.11:17]. God had not changed, neither had the Scriptures. It was Peter's understanding that had changed.

When the Council heard this, they graciously changed their stance, affirming, _"Even to Gentiles God has granted repentance that leads to life"_ [Ac.11:18]. These Gentiles had not repented of their 'Gentileness'. (How could they? As with Jews, that's how they were born.) They were still Gentiles, but now they were affirmed as brothers and sisters in Christ. Family! This Jerusalem Council was a first, albeit cautious, step towards inclusion and beyond. However, whilst they may have said it's okay for local churches to _welcome_ Gentiles, it would take a further Council some years later to finally remove the 'brackets of circumcision' that had continued to be imposed upon Gentile believers by more conservative voices.

To think about...

1. When have you *thought* you were being inclusive only later to realise you weren't?

2. How is the journey to inclusion and beyond like peeling an onion?

3. When have you experienced criticism from more conservative/ traditionalist voices? How did you respond? How would you respond now?

17

Controversy at Council

Acts 15:1-35

"God, who knows the heart, showed that He accepted the Gentiles by giving the Holy Spirit to them, just as He did to us. God did not discriminate between us and them, for He purified their hearts by faith. Now then, why do you try to test God by putting on the necks of Gentiles a yoke that neither we nor our ancestors have been able to bear? No! We believe it is through the grace of our Lord Jesus that we are saved, just as they are.'"
Acts 15:8-11

I've been driving since the age of seventeen and now do it instinctively. I am *that* good at it I no longer need to think about which side of the road I drive on; I just do it. Yes, I pride myself on being a good driver. I confess, the first time I was due to drive in France I was apprehensive; I'd heard stories about cavalier French drivers. Respect to the French though. As I drove along a classic tree-lined road in northern France I was pleased to see that some locals were gracious enough to respect my driving competency by waving at me. I waved back, receiving their praise. To be honest, I could see why my driving competence stood out to them: so many other cars were driving on the right-hand side of the road. They were creating chaos!

What's harder than learning?

Unlearning.

Deeply ingrained and sincerely held habits and beliefs can be difficult to change. Whether through fear, stubbornness, or lack of awareness, we stick to 'what we know', even when the circumstances suggest otherwise. The Acts Church were struggling to unlearn what many of their founders had inherited from their upbringing, customs, culture, and religious thinking.

By Acts 15, Council/ Synod was still debating inclusion, this time whether or not to keep or remove the 'brackets of circumcision'.[83] Those *born* with one identity were attempting to exclude those *born* with a different identity. Jewish-heritage Christians were aghast to hear that Gentile converts, on coming to faith in Jesus Christ, were not then being circumcised, as had been done to them when just eight days old. Circumcision was a physical marking that identified individuals as belonging-by-birth to the ethnic, cultural, political, religious community that was Israel. These 'children of Abraham' were adamant that followers of Christ were still required to uphold the Law and the 'traditional view'. Paul and Barnabas could see that any 'altar call' involving circumcision was going to be a 'hard sell' and unnecessary obstacle to church growth, at least among men. More than that, it denied the all-sufficiency of Christ's saving work [Col.2]. Was justification by faith in Christ enough or did salvation also necessitate adherence to the Mosaic Law? No wonder they found themselves in 'sharp dispute and debate' with the more 'conservative voices' [v.2]. Sound familiar?

Some immediate observations:

1. Though a local matter, with tensions running high, it clearly had wider significance for the whole Church, hence the reason for asking Council/ Synod to consider it [v.2].

2. Representation from churches was welcomed and heard by the Council [v.2-4].

3. The voice of those 'with skin in the game'[84], those 'othered' by the majority view, who had real-life personal stories to tell, were 'in the room' and listened to [v.2].

4. Allies of the excluded, like Peter, Paul, and Barnabas, even eventually James, spoke up [v.7-12].

5. The 'conservatives' who were calling for the 'traditional' line to be upheld were also heard [v.5].

6. In all, there was a lot of listening to one another and to the Holy Spirit. [v.12]

Deeply ingrained, and sincerely held, assertions, based on generations of perceived wisdom take time to change. First, Apostle Peter, and now, Apostle Paul, had changed their minds on what the Scriptures were saying about inclusion. It was taking others much longer.

Recognising the power of story, Peter told his *yet again* (the fourth time in Acts!): how he'd pictured a sheet full of all kinds of impure and unlawful (sinful) to eat animals, reptiles and birds, and then heard a voice from heaven say, 'Catch it. Kill it. Eat it.' His protest had been met with a divine rebuke: *"Do not call anything impure that God has made clean."* Setting an example for us, he then addressed Council as 'Brothers' [v.7]: siblings can debate, even argue; but they remain family. So must we. Maybe Peter was also pointing out this was no abstract, theoretical debate; it had real consequences for those with 'skin in the game'. 'Agree to disagree' is only an option for those with nothing to lose.

The Council had already previously agreed to let local churches accept Gentile converts [v.7; Ac.11:18]. The journey to inclusion and beyond was tortuous. Now, Peter says there is to be no first and second class believers, no 'them' and 'us' [v.8-9]. Why? *"It is through the grace of our Lord Jesus that we are saved"* [v11]. He challenged the inherited 'yoke', or interpretation of Scripture (not God-given Scripture, but human-flawed interpretation of it), that was damaging others. Of course, for them the Scriptures meant, what we now call, the Old Testament. Unlike the 'yoke' of the Pharisees [Mt.23:4], with its burdensome self-justification by laws and customs, the 'yoke' of Jesus – the One who is *the* Way, *the* Truth, and *the* Life – is gentle and liberating [Mt.11:28-30]. It is truly good news!

Having preferred to listen to speakers from all sides, James finally spoke up [v.13]. It was worth the wait! Whilst some today have been very vocal on LGBTQ+ inclusion, many more have remained quiet. Maybe you're one of those who have disciplined themselves to listen to others. Is now, with James, the time for *you* to speak up?

James and the Council went back to the Scriptures [v.15-18]. Though the Scriptures were unchanged, and they had, no doubt, read Amos 9:11-12 many times before, this time they saw something in that passage that they had previously not grasped.

> *"After this I will return and rebuild David's fallen tent. Its ruins I will rebuild, and I will restore it, that the rest of mankind [Edom] may seek the Lord, even all the Gentiles [nations] who bear my name, says the Lord – things known from long ago."* Acts 15:16-18

Whilst Amos spoke of *Edom* seeking the Lord and all *nations* bearing the Lord's name, James realised God's vision was even bigger – it was for all *humanity* and all *Gentiles*. It's not that those who haven't yet affirmed LGBTQ+ inclusion are wrong; it's rather that what they rightly hold so dear – in Christ alone (solus Christus), justification by faith alone (sola fide), acceptance by grace alone (sola gratia), as revealed by Scripture alone (sola scriptura) – is even better than they have realised. It works, not just for some but for all. Amos was an inclusive step; Acts took it to inclusion *and beyond*.

The Scriptures are living and active. For reasons best known to God, now, in response to this pressing situation, the Holy Spirit had highlighted timeless hidden truth – all means ALL. Through a process of listening, respect, theological engagement, and discernment, God had given them a refreshed 'yoke'. We shouldn't be surprised or unsettled by this. It's why we study the likes of systematic theology, hermeneutics, and Church history: to trace the development in our understanding of God and the Scriptures. The Scriptures might not change, but *our* understanding of them does. Acts 15 was another pivotal moment. Far from being the 'slippery slope' to nominalism, it opened the door to the Gospel for the rest of us. You and I are *included* today because of the decision taken at *that* Council meeting.

The Jerusalem Council concluded it was a 'settled matter': *"we should not make it difficult for the Gentiles who are turning to God"* [v.19]. Tragically, for two thousand years, the Church has not delivered on this for LGBTQ+ Gentiles. Despite the intensity of the debate, it's highly unlikely the Council achieved *uniformity*. No doubt some continued to object. And yet, remarkably, the Council did achieve *unity* as they as one came to a collective, albeit conditional, decision, and declared, *"It seemed good to the Holy Spirit and us not to burden you with anything..."* [v.28] What's more, as far as I can see, no-one who disagreed with Council's collective decision left the Church or broke away – at least, not over this issue. When a split did occur, it was over a very human disagreement about policy – which was really about strong personalities [Ac.15:36-41]. There's nothing new under the sun!

Now, back to that conditional blessing. Apostle James declared:

"It is my judgment, therefore that we should not make it difficult for the Gentiles who are turning to God. [20] Instead, we should write to them, telling them to <u>abstain from</u> food polluted by idols, from <u>sexual immorality</u>, from the meat of strangled animals and from blood. [21] For Moses has been preached in every city from the earliest times and is read in every Synagogue on the Sabbath." Acts 15:19-21

Those who start with the belief that homosexuality is wrong seize on this as evidence for their cause; after all it clearly says, 'abstain from sexual immorality'. However, this is a circular argument based on: *homosexuality = sexual immorality*; therefore, *abstain from sexual immorality = abstain from homosexuality*. The text does not mention homosexuality; to infer it does is to impose one's own assumptions, even prejudices.

James and the Council weren't saying Gentiles, having been set free from the Law, could then do whatever, whenever, with whoever. Instead, they, like their Jewish brothers and sisters in Christ, were called to abstain, among other things, from sexual immorality. In the same way, those who are same-sex attracted are under the same obligation as those opposite-sex attracted to abstain from sexual immorality. If the covenant of marriage is seen as the right place for a couple to express their mutual love, commitment, and sexual union, then it would seem disingenuous to deny a gay couple the opportunity to marry, and then accuse them of being sexually immoral because they are not married.

Going deeper, James and the Council were warning the new Gentile believers to break free from pagan temple practices, with their animal sacrifices, prostitution and temple sex slaves. For James, it was a question of *venue*, not just of *menu*.[85] Meat was a luxury only the wealthy could afford on a regular basis. Ordinary Gentiles might only get to eat meat during festivals, and then only as part of temple feasts. Though outside the accepted Canon of Scripture, the likes of Maccabees nevertheless provide an historical insight into the practices and pressures experienced by First Century Judaism:

> *"For the temple was filled with debauchery and revelling by the Gentiles, who dallied with prostitutes and had intercourse with women within the sacred precincts, and besides brought in things for sacrifice that were unfit. The altar was covered with abominable offerings that were forbidden by the laws."* 2 Maccabees 6:4-5

The issue for James and the Council was not the type of meat cut *per se*, rather its source and what the consumer would have been required to do to receive it. The warning was about abstaining from pagan temple practices. If, instead, James had been calling Gentile believers to follow the essence of the Law, he would surely have included keeping the Sabbath. It wasn't that some foods are inherently unclean, whilst others are inherently clean; after all, the Jerusalem Council had already accepted God's Word about foods, *"Do not call anything impure that God has made clean"* [Ac.11:9]. God is not a pedant.

The Acts 15 Council cannot be cited to exclude LGBTQ+ people (it makes no reference to sexuality.) In any case, to be consistent, for this to be applied to homosexuality, all Christians would also be required to abstain from a lot of foods; something that Paul specifically countered elsewhere [1Co.10:25-31].

On the contrary, it's a powerful reminder to us that, though God and the Scriptures are perfect and unchanging, we are not. Sometimes a situation arises that causes us to go back to the Bible to test our 'yoke'. Church history charts this ongoing process from *then* till *now*. We must be humble enough to accept that we have missed or misunderstood something which has always been there, albeit hidden from us until now. This is such an important principle that even God models this humility to us by including it in the Scriptures. My assertion is that the heavy and damaging 'yoke' that has historically used the Bible and God's Name[86] to exclude LGBTQ+ people is now being challenged. It's a holy moment. When God says all, God means ALL, whether gay, straight, bi, or trans; black, brown, or white; young, old, and those 'mutton dressed as lamb'; rich, poor or the 'squeezed middle'; neuro-typical or neuro-diverse... There's even a place for me. And definitely for YOU!

With God, all means ALL.

By now, those readers who began with an affirming/ accepting mindset are likely to feel all the more convinced. Realistically, I accept not everyone will think this. Some who began with a more 'conservative' stance might not have been persuaded by my arguments. I hope it's at least evident that those who take an affirming view do so *because of* – not despite – what they read in the Bible. It would be disingenuous, even mischievous, to claim only one view is based on the Bible. But what do we do when Christians disagree? Who gives way? Paul addresses just this in Romans 14 and 15.

To think about...

1. How is your denomination/ wider church movement responding to LGBTQ+ inclusion? How can or do you participate in this journey to inclusion and beyond?

2. What's more likely, unity or uniformity? What does unity look like?

18

Agree to disagree?

Romans 14:1-23

"Accept the one whose faith is weak, without quar-relling over disputable matters." Romans 14:1-23

Have you ever come to a traffic junction, say in the countryside, where two roads meet, but there are no road markings, no signs? Who has right of way? Who should go? Who should give way? It's easy when there are no other cars on the road. You just do what you want, stop/go as you please; it doesn't really matter. But what happens when another car approaches at the same time as you - from the other side? You want to go *this* way, the other car wants to go *that* way. If you both ignore the other and do your own thing, there'll be a crash. You could both do nothing and just wait. But you could be waiting there for years. That doesn't seem satisfactory either. And so was born the traffic light. (Pub quiz answer: first introduced on 9th December 1868 in London's Parliament Square.)

So now that quiet country lane has traffic lights. When it's 'green' you go, and when it's 'red' you stop. (And when it's 'amber' you 'floor it'?!) This all sounds very straight-forward, harmonious. No more car crashes. What happens when you're at the traffic lights, and you're on 'green' but the other driver is on 'red'? You go, they wait. Imagine if the driver on 'red' says, "I'm on 'red', you should be like me and 'wait' as a I do." It would make no sense. Good drivers are aware of other road users, follow the Highway Code (even 'ambers', yes, you!), and are ultimately responsible for the way *they* drive - not trying to control how others drive. That's what Paul was driving at in Romans chapter 14.

The church in Rome was having some 'car crash' moments – quarrels over disputable matters. Some were seeing 'red' and demanding that everyone stop – stop it. Stop eating meat sacrificed to idols. Stop having fun (especially on Saturdays). Others were seeing 'green'. It's okay to eat any meat. And it's okay to have fun on Saturdays. And Sundays, even on Mondays. Enjoy all of God's gifts.

These were just two examples of 'car crash' quarrels over disputable matters. Paul could have used others. Since then, over the last 2,000 years, we've thought of plenty more. So, Paul sets about helping people with their 'traffic lights', reducing 'car crash' disputes in the Church. We can apply the same principles/ logic to help deal with a myriad of contentious issues we face.

Paul begins, *"Accept the one whose faith is weak, without quarrelling over disputable matters" [Ro.14:1].* If we're held on 'red' we can quickly see 'red mist', we feel our red blood boiling. We lose perspective. A minor hold-up can escalate into 'road rage' – quarrels. The Greek word translated as "disputable matters" is *dialogismōn* (διαλογισμῶν). It's the same word we get 'dialogue' from. They're not so much *disputable* matters, more like debatable, *discussable* matters.

Paul is heading towards Romans 15: *"May the God who gives endurance and encouragement give you a spirit of unity among yourselves as you follow Christ Jesus, so that with one heart and mouth you may glorify the God and*

Father of our Lord Jesus Christ" [Ro.15:5-6]. Paul thinks, though the issues are real, those who find themselves coming from different directions can still co-exist together in unity, in Christ. So, how do we rank disputable matters? Are there degrees of dispute? And who gets to decide?

This matters because some who can't yet affirm same-sex relationships say it's a 'first order' principle. That places it in the highest category of doctrinal significance and a central plank of Christianity. We can test this by adding it to, say, the Apostle's Creed.[87] Does it feel in or out of place when included alongside all the other tenets of the Christian faith? You decide!

I believe in God, the Father almighty,
creator of heaven and earth.
I believe in Jesus Christ, his only Son, our Lord,
who was conceived by the Holy Spirit,
born of the Virgin Mary,
suffered under Pontius Pilate,
was crucified, died, and was buried;
he descended to the dead.
On the third day he rose again;
he ascended into heaven,
he is seated at the right hand of the Father,
and he will come to judge the living and the dead.
I believe in the Holy Spirit,
the holy catholic Church,
the communion of saints,
the forgiveness of sins,
the resurrection of the body,
and the life everlasting.
I believe gay-sex is wrong.

Does that final line fit with the rest of the great doctrinal beliefs? Let's look at this 'first order' claim; it's worth understanding the model.[88]

First-order beliefs are <u>absolutes</u>. They are the non-negotiables of the Christian faith. Take them away and there is no Christianity. They're what ALL Christians believe, be they Anglicans, Baptists, Catholics, Pentecostals, Redeemed Christian Church of God (RCCG), or whatever. For example:

- Belief in the existence of God.

- Belief in the Trinity. One God: Father, Son and Holy Spirit.

- Belief in the Incarnation, saving death, and resurrection of Jesus Christ, God the Son.

Second-order beliefs are <u>convictions</u>. They describe what we and other Christians like us think important – though other Christians may think differently to us. They're often the beliefs that identify us as:

- *Anglican:* Christening of babies; Priest as the mediator between God and people; peculiar to England, Guernsey, Isle of Man, and Jersey, the State Church...

- *Baptist:* believer's baptism; congregational governance; separation of Church and State...

- *Catholic:* Mass becoming the actual body and blood of Christ; veneration of Mary; Papal authority...

- *Pentecostals:* speaking in tongues as the required evidence of being filled with the Holy Spirit...

Third-order beliefs are <u>opinions</u>. Matters of difference between or within our congregations that needn't divide us. Not all Anglican or Baptist churches, for example, take the same stance/ approach on every issue (far from it). It's inevitable, even okay, that not everyone in the same congregation will think the same as everyone else on every issue. For example:

- Different ways of understanding the atonement e.g. Penal, Christus Victor, Moral Influence...

- Different ideas about the end-times and the Second Coming of Christ...

- Different responses to violence and war e.g. Just War, pacifism...

Fourth-order are more like <u>questions</u> – unsettled issues we're all still wrestling with.

But who gets to decide which 'order' a belief or issue is? For example, how do you rank:

- Is there such thing as God? Are we saved through faith in Jesus?

- Baptising *believers* into Christ or christening *babies* into the Church?

- God gives us freewill to make choices or God chooses for us.

- Will there be pets in heaven? Does Heaven's door have a cat flap?

Where do Paul's two examples fit: what can Christians eat, and what can they do on the Sabbath? They're not 'first-order'; Paul says both sides of the argument clearly have faith in Christ. To be 'first order' requires there to be broad and widely accepted consensus. Neither are they 'fourth-order', otherwise there'd be little or no quarrelling/ dispute. It's either 'second-order' or 'third-order'; which might depend on where *you* stand on the issue. What Christians can eat or do on the Sabbath might sound 'third-order'. Dig deeper and what underpins those beliefs could, for some traditionalists, push it into 'second-order', but still nowhere near 'first-order'.

Why does this matter? Because too often we assume everything <u>we</u> believe is 'first-order' – that all others *must* follow/ do. *I believe [this]. I am right. If you don't believe [this], you must be wrong.* Paul says, all that *"I'm on 'red' so you must be too"*, is nonsense.

Back to Paul's contentious issue: whether to eat a pulled pork bap.

Eating 'idol meat' or going 'veggie' was the immediate question. Behind this were the different assumptions and inherited beliefs of Jewish and Gentile Christians. Jewish Christians felt passionately the Old Testament laws should be followed to the letter – even after Christ. Yes, Jesus died to save us, but it says in Leviticus, to stay on the right side of God, you must not sell land, shave off your beard, or get a tattoo. The Gentile Christians felt passionately that Christ had set them free from living under the Law. Grace abounds. It's all about Jesus.

Paul wasn't neutral in this matter. Having changed his view, this was where he *now* landed on this: *"Therefore, there is now no condemnation for those who are in Christ Jesus, because through Christ Jesus the law of the Spirit who gives life has set you free from the law of sin and death." [Ro.8:1-2].* For a Jew, eating certain prescribed meats was horrific, vile. More than that, it was unlawful. It was <u>sinful</u>. Hence the shock of Peter's dream and change of attitude in Acts 10. He saw Heaven opened. Lots of forbidden animals. And heard a voice saying, *Catch it. Kill it. Eat it.* Paul was also clear, on this issue, he was on 'green': *"I am convinced, being fully persuaded in the Lord Jesus, that <u>nothing is unclean in itself</u>." [Ro.14:14]* After all, Jesus had said, *"Nothing that enters a person from the outside can make them 'unclean'" [Mk.7:18].* Paul thought their argument weak. It denied the sufficiency of Jesus; Christ is <u>all</u> you need. So, he made the following points:

Accept others - Don't judge.

Just as Jesus had said, *"Do not judge, or you too will be judged" [Mt.7:1],* so Paul was emphatic: *"Why do you judge your brother or sister? Or why do you treat them with contempt? For we will all stand before God's judgment seat"*

[Ro.14:10]. Again, *"Let us stop passing judgment on one another"* [*Ro.14:13]*. Instead, *"Accept one another just as Christ accepted you"* *[Ro.15:7]*. It is the Holy Spirit's job to convict of right and wrong, and to reveal truth, not ours.

Allow others - Don't impose your view.

"Let us stop passing judgment on one another. Instead, make up your mind not to put any stumbling block or obstacle in the way of a brother or sister." [Ro.14:13] No-one was saying ALL Christians must now eat meat. Instead, Paul says, if your 'take' on faith does *not* allow you to eat meat, don't eat it; go vegetarian or vegan. And if, like Paul, your 'take' on faith *does* allow you to eat meat, similarly, you are free to tuck into your pulled pork bap. You can 'agree to disagree' by ensuring the 'church lunch' provides both meat and meat-free options. Imagine the uproar if, having said "let's agree to disagree", the Gentile Christians had insisted only meat was served, with the meat-free option denied to the Jewish Christians! Paul says, what we must <u>not</u> do is force others to abide by our approach. You are responsible for what you believe; let others be responsible for their beliefs.

Paul's logic helps us with this other debatable matter: same-sex relationships. To what extent can a Christian be gay? What about same-sex marriage? As with Old Testament food laws, some Christians believe same-sex relationships are sinful. They're on 'red' with that. A growing number of Evangelicals, who love the same God, are filled with the same Holy Spirit, and who read and seek to live by the same Bible, are on 'green' for this. For them, it's about a monogamous, faithful and loving relationship between two people, whatever their gender or sexuality. Following Paul's logic, if your 'take' on faith does not allow/ permit same-sex relationships or same-sex marriage, you are <u>free</u> *not* to enter one. And, if your take on faith *does* allow you to have one, you are <u>free</u> to do so. What we must *not* do is force others to abide by our individual approach. We mustn't put any stumbling block or obstacle in the way of our gay, lesbian, bi, trans, or queer siblings in Christ.

This requires significant grace and mutual respect. Those who are LGBTQ+ are asking to co-exist in the Church, alongside their heterosexual siblings. They're not asking churches to stop marrying opposite-sex couples; they're simply asking that the same freedom be granted to all, whether 'straight' or 'gay'. Not reciprocating this grace, many 'conservatives/ traditionalists' insist that only heterosexual marriage is permissible. I find it astonishing how they fail to see this disparity in their one-sided version of 'agree to disagree'. One advocates freedom for all; the other, freedom for just some. They'd do well to heed Jesus' words: *"Do to others what you would have them do to you"* [Mt.7:12]. Imagine the uproar if the debate was settled by only permitting same-sex marriage, with all heterosexual couples denied the opportunity of "tying the knot"? Paul in Romans 14 calls for a more generous approach to those we disagree with.

At a denominational Church level, this means having the grace to accept that some member churches will be LGBTQ+ affirming and so registered for both opposite-sex and same-sex marriage; and some member churches won't – both true to their convictions, neither denying the other their freedom. The Methodist Church in the UK adopted this principle in 2021.[89] It gives freedom to all local Methodist congregations and ministers to marry same-sex couples, whilst also giving them all equal freedom not to do so if their conscience does not allow. As a result, some Methodist churches do, others don't – but they all remain Methodist churches together. They're modelling Romans 14 for other denominations to follow.

At a local level, a congregation that authentically seeks to 'agree to disagree' will register to conduct *both* opposite-sex *and* same-sex marriages. There is grace in permitting others to pursue the freedom that we ourselves don't feel we have. Only this ensures all people can exercise their freedom. Providing for 'straight' couples, but not for queer couples is *not* 'agreeing to disagree'; it is privileging the majority at the expense of the minority – something Paul was specifically challenging. An alternative 'agree to disagree' approach would be for the church to not marry anyone, be they 'straight' or queer. All couples could be directed to marry at the Register Office. This would have some integrity in that it prohibited all, but would weaken the church's perceived commitment to marriage.

Accept yourself - Don't deny God's work in you.

Be confident in what you believe - *and why*. *"Each one should be fully convinced in their own mind." [Ro.14:5]*. It's okay to think you're right, especially if it comes from rigorous, open, humble investigation. *"Do not allow what you consider good to be spoken of as evil." [v.16] "Blessed is the one who does not condemn himself by what he approves." [v.23]*. Be open and confident in how God is leading you, how God has wired you to be. That may be different to the way others understand things. If you think your reasoning is the stronger, don't put any stumbling block or obstacle in your brother's or sister's way *[v.13]*.

Don't flaunt your freedom in front of the weaker

The tough part is to be gracious to those who think differently to us. If they are so weak, they can't cope when someone eats a sausage roll in their presence, or is just a bit too *gay*, be secure in how God has wired you to be, and the sexuality God has gifted you – be that straight or gay – and don't cause them to stumble. But equally, remain true to the grace Christ has given us. Yes, Gentile Christians weren't to flaunt their freedom in Christ, but neither were they to deny that freedom won by Christ on the Cross and slip back to being law-rooted Jewish believers.

Don't presume it's always others who must give way. Paul says, if you believe your way of thinking about 'this' is strong, that you're in the right (and, let's be honest, most 'conservatives/ traditionalists' believe they are!), then Paul says, for the sake of unity and to alleviate the distress of others, *you* should be willing to lay down your privilege on this disputable, discussable matter. When you do, you show your *true* strength. Shouting the loudest can be a sign of weakness or low confidence.

Those who can't yet affirm same-sex relationships presumably do so because the Biblical case, in *their* opinion, is weak. They are convinced by the strength of their own reasoning and in the weakness of others; as far as they are concerned, they are right, everyone else is wrong. Therefore, for the sake of the straight majority, they expect the LGBTQ+ minority to drop the call for inclusion. Yet, following Paul's logic, if they are so convinced by the strength of their view and the weakness of the queer case, then 'conservatives/ traditionalists' should *"make every effort to do what leads to peace"* [v.19] by accepting those they consider weak, without passing judgment on this disputable matter or putting a stumbling block or obstacle in their sibling's way [v.13]. Those who can't yet affirm same-sex relationships might not agree with their LGBTQ+ siblings but it causes them no harm, so why continue to object? Straight people aren't being denied what they are or who they love; nor are they experiencing the higher rates of anxiety, depression, self-harm or even suicide that collectively LGBTQ+ people are. Not all stumbling blocks or obstacles are equal.

It turns out, the sin is not the meat eating; it's having your beliefs and behaviours out of line: saying one thing but doing another. Thinking and acting in silos – not having a systematic theology: *"Whoever has doubts is condemned if they eat, because their eating is not from faith; and everything that does not come from faith is sin."* [v.23].

> ### To think about...
> 1. Which 'doctrinal order' do you think best fits LGBTQ+ inclusion? Why?
>
> 2. What does 'agree to disagree' look like in your church? To what extent is it equally applied? What needs to change?

19

String and rubber bands

Romans 15:1-13

"Accept one another, then, just as Christ accepted you, in order to bring praise to God." Romans 15:1-13

As a new Christian with no prior church experience, I was told it was all about Jesus, yet I seemed to hear far more about Paul and his 'after the event' explanations of Christ. Church in the mid-1980s and 1990s appeared dominated by 'Pauline theology'; only 'social Gospel' types bringing it back to Jesus. Then, with the new Millennium, the pendulum swung back to a re-discovery of the radical Jesus. Now, we seem to have a healthier perspective of Paul in relation to Jesus. As Christians, we interpret the whole of Scripture, from Genesis to Revelation, through the revelation (lens) of Christ, *the* Word (Logos) of God. Called a Christo-centric hermeneutic, it's a 'fancy pants' way of saying, it is Jesus who makes sense of Paul (and Abraham, Moses, Ruth..), not Paul who makes sense of Jesus.

Paul had been born into the Jewish tradition; he was steeped in, what we now call, the Old Testament. As a leading Pharisee, he was an expert in the Law. For him, it was all about Israel, God's privileged elect, and justifying yourself by keeping on the right side of God's laws, sacrifices and festivals. But then, he encountered Jesus. Scales fell from his eyes, he now saw his hitherto 'blind spots'. God was generous, open, full of grace, mercy and love; albeit, with some strong words to say to religious uptight people that used their twist on religion to exclude or put others down. How could his life ever be the same? He devoted himself to opening up this Gospel to ALL, be they Jewish or Gentile, whoever.

Paul was clearly a brilliant mind, forensic in the way he established his case for Christ. No wonder his letters are so packed full of meaning. Romans, in particular, is a magnificent explanation of the Gospel, the good news of Jesus. If Matthew, Mark, Luke and John are the *what*, Romans is the *why*. You can read it in just 30-35 minutes, yet Dr Martyn Lloyd-Jones famously spent 10 years preaching through it, verse by verse. Every sentence is packed full of meaning.

The Church in Rome was faced with some strong opinions, some mutually exclusive. For example, Christians had different 'takes' on food laws and the Sabbath. Because we all learn differently, and sometimes the unexpected can give us fresh insight, we're going to dial-up the *visual* and *kinaesthetic* with some string and a ball of multi-coloured rubber bands. Pause and go find a piece of string and a rubber band.

First, the string...

> **Task>** **Take a piece of string and try to stretch it.** What are its limitations?

Jewish Christians were all cut from the same *string*. They had come to believe they – and they alone – were God's chosen, the Elect. They felt passionately that those who follow Christ should still observe the Old

Testament laws – all of them. Regarding food, they quoted Leviticus 11 and Deuteronomy 14:

- Only eat mammals with split hooves that chew the cud. So, beef, lamb, and goat were permitted. But *not* pork, because pigs don't chew, they just swallow. Greedy pigs! Or, in case you're tempted, camel, because, though they have toes, they aren't each split.

- Chicken, turkey, duck, and goose were acceptable (The Victorian-era Christmas lunch was looking good), but ostrich, sea gull and vultures, were strictly off menu.

- Fish with fins and scales were allowed, but not shellfish (no prawn sandwich.[90])

- All reptiles, amphibians and insects were forbidden, but four kinds of locusts were permitted (so, a limited *I'm A Celebrity Get Me Out of Here* bushtucker trial.)

- No mixing of meat and dairy – so no cheeseburgers.

- And, how and where the animal was slaughtered was very specific; all the blood from the animal had to be drained.

Just as there is no 'give' in string, so there was no 'give' in Jewish Christians' approach to the Law. They said, if you can't be 100% certain of the meat's provenance, just eat vegetables. They believed it wasn't only distasteful or even cruel to animals to break these food laws; it was <u>sinful</u>. For them, it was a matter of avoiding sin and God's judgement, choosing instead holiness. They were also concerned not to eat idolatrous meat that stemmed from pagan sacrifices.

Before anyone rushes to criticise them, by the time of the Roman Occupation, what you ate marked you out as Jewish. To break their spirit, the Roman oppressors would force the Jewish population to eat pork. Keeping the food laws was a sign of their:

- *identity* and self-respect – who they were;

- *defiance* against Roman oppression;

- *devotion* to God.

Upholding the Jewish food laws was a courageous act of defiance against the Roman invaders, and of identification with God.

> **Task>** **Tie the string around a few pens/ pencils.** How secure are they? What happens if you later try to slip in more pens/ pencils to the collection? What prevents you from adding more pens/ pencils? Where does that leave the rest of the pens/ pencils? How might this illustrate the limitations of the Law, as sometimes portrayed in the Bible?

Now for the rubber bands

[Pub Quiz bonus: When was the first rubber band introduced?[91]]

> **Task>** **Take a rubber band from the ball and stretch it; feel how different it is to the string.** What can it do that the string could never do?

Just as, when it burst on the scene, the rubber band was revolutionary and yet quickly made perfect sense, so Jesus came with His revolutionary 'take' (yoke) on the Law and God. In His hands, the Law didn't seem as rigid; there was flex.

> **Task>** **Hold the ball of multi-coloured rubber bands and note the number, size and colours of the bands.**

Jesus' Gospel was good news for *everyone*, Gentiles as well as Jews. Just as a ball of multi-coloured rubber bands contains rubber bands of all sizes and colours, so Paul came to realise that God's Kingdom is for ALL people (not just Jewish people) and ALL nations (not just Israel). It is gloriously diverse!

Task> **See how many more pens, pencils and other items your rubber band can accommodate!** Feel the stretch and the inevitable tension. How comfortable do you feel with that tension? What would be the result if your priority was to reduce tension?

A rubber band comes into its own when it is *stretched*. It was never meant to hold just *one* pen, but <u>lots</u> of them – all different kinds, shapes, sizes. Jesus demonstrated that God's Kingdom stretches to include those others excluded: women, children, socially/ religiously 'unclean' shepherds, the poor, oppressors, religious law breakers, those with stigmatising diseases, and those bluntly written-off as "sinners". All those previously excluded found this grace stretched to include them too. It stretches for YOU too. Through our mission and ministry, displayed through the words, works and wonders of Christ, we seek to see God's Kingdom stretched to include ever more people. That's why we pray, *"Your Kingdom come, Your will be done, on earth as it is in Heaven..."*

Inevitably, stretch leads to *tension*. That can feel unnerving. Gentile Christians were saying, 'go with the stretch'; this is what God's Kingdom is all about. And they were right. Christ had fulfilled the Law, He had set them free from it and they were now at liberty to eat anything. It was no longer about you and what you did or did not eat; it was all about Christ and what He has done, once and for all. Pure grace!

Task> **Stretch your rubber band to breaking point.** How far do you have to go before it snaps? More or less than you expected?

Jewish Christians were saying, if you deviate too far, it'll *snap*. And they were right too. If you stretch beyond the given limitations, it <u>*will*</u> snap. Paul was <u>*not*</u> saying (and neither am I), anything goes; do whatever you like. God's Kingdom, like all kingdoms, has boundaries. There is a right way to live and that's the radical way of Jesus.

Some prefer a more rigid approach – the certainty can feel comforting – but that's more likely to break. Sin is not so much a list of rules that have been broken, rather a broken state of relationship that goes way beyond specific offences. The Law couldn't – and can't – bring us back into right relationship with God, only Jesus – through His sacrificial life, death and resurrection – can do that.

> **Task>** **Having stretched the rubber band, release the tension, and watch it ping back.**

We have all inherited experiences, beliefs, attitudes, assumptions that are our default position. We get them from our upbringing, culture, church tradition, communities, media... They can be subtle yet very powerful. Sometimes, the Holy Spirit stretches us and our thinking in ways that are counter-cultural to what we have inherited or the spaces we inhabit. Don't be surprised, when we are stretched, there is an in-built pressure to ping-back. Statements of inclusion can be agreed relatively quickly; achieving genuine and lasting culture change takes far longer. It's building up inclusive 'muscle memory' so that, in that split-second moment, our instinctive response is one of grace and inclusion, not judgment and exclusion. It takes prolonged and repeated stretch before the 'rubber band' learns to embrace its new 'settled position'.

> **Task>** **Turn a rubber band inside out and, whilst it's stretched (eg around a box), use a <u>fine</u>-tip pen to write on it, *All means ALL*. Let the rubber band ping-back and turn it back.** How is this like a hidden message? What would you have to do to reveal it?

When I first used this illustration, I spent hours the night before, writing this hidden message – "All means ALL" – on the inside of every rubber band. As I squinted with the pen, I prayed over each one. These were the bands my congregation used for this exercise. Only at the end of the service did I nudge them to look for a hidden message. Gradually, voices began to shout out. They were only starting to see what had always been there from the beginning, but which they had, for whatever reason, missed until this point. Only as the rubber bands were stretched, and with a mix of prompt and curiosity, did the message become clear: All means ALL. It was a powerful moment.

Stretch can lead to revelation. Maybe it's only then that we become willing to consider other possibilities beyond the familiar. The Bible is full of 'stretch moments' that led to greater understanding. For God, it was never just about Israel and the Jewish nation; it was always about ALL people, ALL nations. You, me, and everyone.

> *"For everything that was written in the past was written to teach us, so that through the endurance taught in the Scriptures and the encouragement they provide we might have hope."* Romans 15:4

Scripture might not change, but our understanding of it sometimes does. That's why Jesus frequently said, "You have *heard* it said... But *I* tell you..." He had come, not to *replace* the Law, but to *fulfil* it. Paul wanted the Jewish Christians to know that God had included Jews <u>and</u> Gentiles. So, he quoted four times from the Old Testament, covering the Law, Prophets, and Writings:

1. **David**, though King of Israel, says: *"Therefore I will praise you among the Gentiles; I will sing the praises of your name."* [Ro.15:9; 2Sam.22:40] Where? Among the Gentiles - those who don't follow the Law.

2. ***Moses*** says, *"Rejoice, you Gentiles, with his people."* [Ro.15:10; Deut. 32:43]

3. ***Psalmist*** says: *"Praise the Lord, all you Gentiles; let all the peoples extol him."* [Ro.15:11; Ps.117:1]

4. ***Isaiah*** says: *"The Root of Jesse will spring up, one who will arise to rule over the nations; in him the Gentiles will hope."* [Ro.15:12; Isa.11:10]

Jewish-heritage Christians had been struggling to accept the new Gentile Christians, with their fresh 'take' on faith. Paul was clear, the Gentiles weren't just to be tolerated; they were to be celebrated and affirmed as those beautifully and equally made in the image of God.

Whilst Abraham and Lot had split over their differences, Paul urged Jewish and Gentile believers to look instead at what united them, seeing those you disagree with as Christ sees them:

> **"May the God who gives endurance and encouragement give you the same attitude of mind toward each other that Christ Jesus had."** *Romans 15:5*

It's the same language he uses in Philippians 2:

> **"Do nothing out of selfish ambition or vain conceit. Rather, in humility value others above yourselves, not looking to your own interests but each of you to the interests of the others. In your relationships with one another, have the same mindset as Christ Jesus: who, being in very nature God, did not consider equality with God something to be used to his own advantage; rather, he made himself nothing by taking the very**

nature of a servant, being made in human likeness. And being found in appearance as a man, he humbled himself by becoming obedient to death – even death on a cross!" Philippians 2:3-8

Paul says to the Jewish Christians: you follow Christ; so, follow Him, do what Christ does. And to the Gentile Christians, Paul says: you follow Christ; so, follow Him, do what Christ does. What does Christ do? He lays down His rights, His power, His life, for us. Christ, who was the ultimate strong, became, for our sake, the ultimate weak. We who are strong (including strong in our convictions), for the sake of others, are to exercise our freedom Christ's way.

Paul calls for _unity_ (grouping around Christ), not *uniformity* (grouping around people like us). Christian unity is not found in Christians but in Christ. Families don't always agree. Yes, our differences can be real (we all think we're right), but what's far bigger than any other 'label' we carry is what it means to be family – siblings in Christ. If you are a child of God, and I am a child of God, then we are brothers/ sisters. We are family.

It's not just *unity* of thought, it's a _spirit_ *of unity* [v.5]. It comes straight from the heart of God. At the core of God is Unity: Father, Son, and Holy Spirit co-existing together.

When we see Christ in each other, then we – despite our differences – worship *with ONE heart and ONE mouth*. When we show the same attitude of mind toward each other that Christ Jesus had, then *"with one mind and one voice we glorify the God and Father of our Lord Jesus Christ"* [v.6]. No wonder Paul says, *"Accept one another, then, just as Christ accepted you, in order to bring praise to God"* [v.7].

He concludes by saying to those who struggle to accept one another: *"May the God of hope fill you with all joy and peace as you trust in him, so that you may overflow with hope by the power of the Holy Spirit"* [v.13].

20

Wonderfully made!

Psalm 139

"I praise you because I am fearfully and wonderful-ly made; your works are wonderful, I know that full well." Psalm 139:14

In 1983 I had just discovered both God and music. It was the year the iconic compilation album, *Now That's What I Call Music*, came out. This double-sided vinyl album pulled together a mix of *artists* (Duran Duran, Phil Collins, U2, Culture Club, The Cure, UB40...), *music genres* (futurist, pop, rock, reggae, ballads...), and *themes*. It seemed, there was a track for every mood. In the Bible, Psalms is like a compilation album – *Now That's What I Call Psalms* ; 150 psalms, pulling together a mix of writers (David, Asaph, The Sons of Korah[92], Solomon...), genres, and themes. What's more, it seems, there's a Psalm for every mood or situation.

Many Christians find Psalm 139 a deep source of encouragement and affirmation. Written by David (long after the Fall), it's organised into four sections, each with six verses. Twenty-six times David says of God, *You: You* made me; *You* know me; *You* discern me (You 'get' me); *You* are here for me. Pause and read it now.

Of course, this Psalm, like all of Scripture, was not written just for straight, cis people, but for *everyone*, irrespective of their sexuality or gender identity. Read it again, twice. Imagine reading it through the 'lens' of someone who is opposite-sex attracted. Then, read it again, through the 'lens' of someone who is same-sex attracted. What do you notice? What does it stir in you?

God knows us (v.1-6)

God knows us better than we know ourselves [v.1]. Through our 'lived experiences', interactions with others, moments of refection, and listening to God, we spend a lifetime discovering who we *really* are; how God has 'wired' us. Whilst others might only see the surface-level version of ourselves that we choose to reveal, God has uniquely, completely searched us, inside and out. There is no hiding from God [v.2-3]. God sees us at our best and at our worst. When the One who *Sees All, Knows All*, is the Source of all Love [1Jn.4:8], to be so *known* feels wonderful [v.6]. God *sees* us, even if others around us do not.

In a hetero-normative world, no one need 'come out' as straight or cis. For them, it's just how things are. Yet, for those who are lesbian, gay, bi or trans, 'coming out' is a defining moment (or succession of moments), often packed with conflicting emotions, and reactions from others. Though vocalising one's identity can be empowering, no one ever need 'come out' to God [v.4]. Long before any of us had any awareness of our sexual orientation or gender identity, whether straight or gay, God already knew.

God is everywhere (v.7-12)

Even if we're in denial about our 'true self' or seeking to evade others or God, we can run but not hide. God is everywhere. Verse 8 reminds us that, whilst God is in the obvious 'holy' places, God is also found where we least expect (or want.) The Bible often uses the 'depths of the sea' to symbolise chaos, those places or points in our life where we feel least in control of ourselves or our surroundings. And yet, even there/ then, God is with us. Sometimes there are both 'push' and 'pull' factors: we are *pushed* away from familiar spaces we no longer feel safe in because of the attitudes of individuals or institutions; we are *pulled* towards unfamiliar spaces we find safe because of the attitudes of individuals or communities. Looking back, through the best and worst of times, do you now see that some*thing* or some*one*, God, was guiding/ protecting/ nudging you [v.10]?

Love how God has wired you (v.13-18)

Sexuality is *part* of our identity, our 'inmost being'. Whilst some still debate *nature* or *nurture*, verse 13 says it's *neither*. God – not you, not others – created your 'inmost being'. That includes our sexuality. Our sexual orientation, be that gay or straight, is neither an accident nor 'lifestyle *choice*'. It is part of how we are wired – how we were created – by God! It applies equally to all, whatever our sexuality.

How liberating to be able to agree with God that *you* are, indeed, *"fearfully and wonderfully made"* [v.14]. Not in any way error, not even just acceptable, but *wonderful!* Not just your word, your truth, but *God's* Word, God's Truth.

Many lesbian, gay, bi, trans, and queer people 'come out' and never look back. They know they're aligned with how God has wired them to be. Nevertheless, others have also experienced a lifetime of homophobia or transphobia, which has left them with strong feelings of shame and self-loathing. They feel far from wonderful. Tragically, much of that shame has come from those who claim to represent God. It is they who are unaligned with God.

"I praise you because I am fearfully and wonderfully made; your works are wonderful, I know that full well." [v.14]. You know this, but do you really *know?* This truth is not just for heterosexual cis people. To what extent do you fully believe it applies equally to those who are LGBTQ+? To what extent do you praise God because of your *sexuality* (whatever that is) and how God has wired you to be? Do you allow others to do the same?

Jesus said, *"Love your neighbour as yourself"* [Mt.22:36-39]. Whilst we all know people who appear to be in love with themselves, we also know others who struggle with self-love.

Whilst we each inherit human genetic code, having been "knitted together" by biological parents/ carriers [v.13], there is a far bigger truth – we are each made in the image of God [Ge.1:27]. What God has made, is not just good, it's <u>very</u> good [Ge.1:31]. Similarly, Paul said, *"We are God's handiwork"* [Eph.2:10]. That makes each of us inherently, whatever our sexuality, a priceless art treasure, a true and unique masterpiece. God has invested His own personality into you: His creativity, joy, patience, attention to detail, love, and so forth. And it's not just you.

When it comes to gender identity (different to sexual orientation), we are reminded here that some experience the trauma of gender dysphoria – acute distress when there's a mismatch between their biological sex (as labelled binarily at birth) and their gender identity. Fundamentalists suggest that, to question or change gender identity goes against what God has declared 'wonderful'. But this overlooks God's unique insight. The Psalmist says, *"Your eyes saw my <u>unformed body</u>"* [v.16]. God alone sees us, imagines us, before we have biological bodies, with labelled sex. God alone sees our *true self* or 'inmost being'; which is not defined by the temporary tent-like shelters which we call our physical bodies [2Co.5:1]. In any case, fundamentalists would then have to admit, in light of modern medical breakthroughs of IVF and gestational surrogacy, God is not the only Knitter. Beware selective literal dysfunction!

Yield to God (v.19-24)

The Psalmist gets angry at all the injustices, the mistreatment of God's wonderful masterpieces, the 'blood thirsty' violence – physical, emotional, psychological, sexual, even spiritual – so rife in fractured life. The Psalmist wants to lash out in revenge [v.19]. What's more, the violent ones falsely claim *they* have God on their side. *"They speak of you with evil intent; your adversaries misuse your name"* [v.20] The Third Commandment [Ex.20 :7] is much less about don't say "OMG"; it's far more about, don't claim God's authority (Name) to justify your own attitudes or behaviours. How often have we seen the Bible used as a weapon to attack or demonise communities? Too often, queer people have experienced hatred and violence in all its myriad forms from some 'glass half empty' individuals and institutions using God's Name to justify their own ignorance or intolerance. If *they* say it, it sounds homophobic; if *God* says it, it must be true. And this only gets the Psalmist even more angry. #NotInGodsName.

Then the Psalmist remembers, 'when they go low, we go high'. The Jesus Way is radical non-violence, it's love. So, yield to God's agenda: *"Search me, God, and know my heart; test me and know my anxious thoughts. See if there is any offensive way in me, and lead me in the way everlasting"* [v.23-24].

To think about...

1. Think about what makes you.. you. How are *you* 'fearfully and wonderfully made'? Does this apply to those who are 'straight'? Does it apply equally to those who are gay?

2. What does it mean for you to *yield* to God?

21

Culture wars

"Therefore, I urge you, brothers and sisters, in view of God's mercy, to offer your bodies as a living sacrifice, holy and pleasing to God – this is your true and proper worship. Do not conform to the pattern of this world, but be transformed by the renewing of your mind. Then you will be able to test and approve what God's will is – his good, pleasing and perfect will." Romans 12:1-2

Psalm 139 offers a profound challenge to those who defend so-called 'conversion therapies'. Many 'conservatives/ traditionalists' believe sexual *orientation* (as opposed to sexual *attraction*) is a myth. At the very least, they are sceptical about the last 150 years of scientific research.[93] They think it's just down to personal choice, a 'lifestyle preference', encouraged by the erosion of social and cultural heterosexual norms (fuelled by progressive liberal arts, education, media, and politics.) Some – curiously, aligning themselves with Sigmund Freud – speculate that same-sex attraction is the result of childhood trauma, sexual violence, absence of a father figure, or presence of a domineering mother. In short, they think it's *nurture*, not *nature*.

Whatever, they see it as *sin*, a profound offence to God. It is this root belief that drives their conviction that, like a disease or affliction, same-sex attraction can be cured or removed; as if, with the right treatment or prayer, a person can be healed or delivered from their 'gayness'. An array of so-called 'conversion therapies', ranging from electric shock treatment, hormonal castration, ingesting 'purifying' substances, intense and prolonged sessions of prayer and fasting (or enforced starvation), to the deliverance of evil spirits and demon possession (and even, at horrific extreme, 'corrective rape'), have all been used to try and change people's sexual orientation or gender identity. There is no credible evidence that such 'treatments' have any effect on changing sexuality.

Victims of this abuse (let's call it for what it is) speak of being demonised, made to feel profoundly unclean, dirty, and powerless. Survivors speak out courageously about the physical, psychological, emotional, social, and spiritual hurt and long-term damage such treatments have had on them. No wonder there is such a strong move to ban 'conversion therapies', despite opposition from conversative voices. Tragically, society, even the Church, has 'form'. Previous generations sought to cure those afflicted by the 'curse' of left-handedness in ways that rendered them traumatised – and still left-handed![94] Of course, this is classic 'majority culture' power play.

Sociology 101 reminds us that culture is the summation of 'how life is', as understood *and defined* by those in the majority. It's what passes for 'normal' and is expressed through shared attitudes, behaviour, beliefs, conventions, language, rules, and symbols. Its aim is always to maintain the *status quo*, thus prolonging its dominant position. Culture is learnt and passed on to successive generations through a process of socialisation, using a mix of subtle and unsubtle rewards and punishments. Those who uphold the 'norm' are included, valued, provided for (rewarded), whereas those who deviate from the 'norm' find themselves excluded, talked-down, overlooked (punished). Given that the majority (90%) of people are right-handed, it's not surprising the 'norm' designs computer keyboards, guitars, microwave doors, scissors, swipe-card machines, tape measures, and so on (try it), that *reward* being right-handed, therefore *punishing* deviant left-handers.

Inevitably, not everyone is able or willing to conform to the 'norm'. As individuals push-back and find each other, they form their own sub-culture – with their own 'norm'. In defiance of the majority, they now have their own attitudes, behaviour, beliefs, conventions, language, rules, and symbols. The majority culture is always threatened by minority sub-cultures. To protect the status quo and its privileged position of power, the majority culture doubles-down on its rewards and punishments to crush the deviant threat. If that doesn't work, it switches tack and looks instead to adopt the deviant sub-culture – or at least, a tamer, more moderate version of it – as its own. Whilst the majority culture dislikes change, it hates losing power and control even more, and so embraces its 'new norm'. Change in mainstream culture only happens through the challenge of sub-cultures.

Just as majority culture defines 'normal' as being right-handed, so it says the 'norm' is to be cis 'straight'. In the 2021 Census, 89.4% of the UK population aged 16+ identified as straight or heterosexual.[95] Anyone else is deemed 'deviant'. Just look at the strength of push back from 'conservative/ traditionalist' voices hell-bent on maintaining the status quo and their privilege position of power. Some conservative churches (often wealthier), including Anglican and Baptist, are protesting their opposition to same-sex inclusion by withholding their financial obligations to their denomination or diocese. It's a classic reward and punishment strategy, that sails close to 'simony' [Ac.8:18]. These same 'conservative' voices have collectively been somewhat muted or silent on women's justice, racial justice, disability justice, environmental justice...

Church history provides invaluable insights into the process of change. Change doesn't happen because those in the majority decide to change.

Remember, the mission is: "protect the *status quo*". Instead, change happens when those labelled 'heretical' (the theological equivalent of deviant) see something missed by the majority and push for change. The Roman Empire sought to maintain the *status quo* by punishing the new radical Christ-following sect – with all its love, peace, justice, grace – and rewarding those who continued to declare 'Caesar is Lord'. Yet, when those Christian radicals became unstoppable, as more and more turned to Christ, to hold on to its position of power, the Roman Empire switched tack, and adopted Christianity as its own. Under Emperor Constantine (306-337 AD), it conceded limited ground in order to retain its overall dominance. This is a pattern repeated throughout church history. Some, once judged heretical, find themselves then on the margins of orthodoxy, before eventually breaking through to become mainstream – the 'norm'. It's not long before these 'pioneers become settlers' as they, in turn, then resist new radical movements. Conservatives' appeal to church tradition fails to recognise that Church history is on-going, never static.

Martin Luther (1483-1546), John Calvin (1509-1564), Ulrich Zwingli (1484-1531), and Thomas Cranmer (1489-1556) – all heroes of the Reformation – were once labelled 'revisionists' for their radical commitment to the whole of Scripture (sola Scriptura) and opening-up faith in Jesus to all. Luther was excommunicated by the Church, Cranmer burnt at the stake for heresy, but the tide had turned. Ironically, now it appears sections of Protestantism are once again resisting the cry of *sola Scriptura* to protect the *status quo*.

Faced with pressure to change, some 'conservatives/ traditionalists' are adopting a tamer version of same-sex attraction as their acceptable face of inclusion. Organisations like Living Out[96] and True Freedom Trust[97] maintain that being gay is *not* a sin, but having gay sex *is*. Whilst looking to support, and advocate for, Christians who are same-sex attracted, they nevertheless maintain the 'conservative' line that sex can only be between a man and woman in heterosexual marriage. With notes of coercive control, they teach abstinence and life-long singleness as the only acceptable response. After all, didn't Jesus say, *"Whoever wants to be my disciple must deny themselves and take up their cross and follow me. For whoever wants to save their life will lose it, but whoever loses their life for me will find it."* [Mt.16:2425]? Deny your sexuality for the sake of Christ; it's the cross LGBTQ+ must bear.

This is surely an example of 'confirmation bias': looking for 'evidence' to support one's pre-existing assumptions or prejudices. Imagine I inherit or promote the strong belief that having 20/20 near-perfect eyesight is a sign of holiness, and, therefore, that those who must wear prescription glasses are sinful. Then I open my Bible and read, *"The eye is the lamp of the body. If your eyes are healthy, your whole body will be full of light. But if your eyes are unhealthy, your whole body will be full of darkness. If then the light within you is darkness, how great is that darkness!"* [Mt.6:22-23]. Boom! Confirmation: *the Bible says* glass-wearers are sinners. Yes, love those with weak eyesight, but hate their sinful lifestyle-choice of wearing glasses. You would rightly say I was misusing Scripture to justify my own prejudice and intolerance. The Bible's mention of 'sexual immorality' can too easily be used as evidence to support pre-existing assumptions or prejudices about what constitutes 'sexual immorality'. Imagine someone believes it sexually immoral to wear elasticated-waist trousers. They might feel vindicated by the likes of Romans 13:13, Galatians 5:19, and Revelation 9:21, but it would simply be conformation bias.

Paul says, *"Do not conform to the pattern of this world, but be transformed by the renewing of your mind"* [Ro.12:2]. Because of the presumptions they start with, some of those who oppose LGBTQ+ inclusion cite this for their cause. Yet, we can equally say, don't 'conform to the pattern of this world', with its homophobia and oppression towards lesbian, gay, bi, trans, or queer communities. Confirmation bias is the scourge of all who seek to take the Bible seriously – hence the need for critical self-reflection as we engage with the whole of Scripture.

Abstinence organisations, like True Freedom Trust and Living Out, turn what, for a few people – whether straight or gay – is the spiritual *gift* of celibacy [1Co.7:7], into a mandatory requirement for all same-sex attracted people. Then it feels less a gift, more a life sentence. Anyone who feels called by God to live celibately must surely be respected; it's an honourable decision. And yet God gives us all different gifts [Ro.12:6]. Paul says, *"If your gift is prophesying, then prophesy in accordance with your faith; if it is serving, then serve; if it is teaching, then teach; if it is to encourage, then give encouragement; if it is giving, then give generously; if it is to lead, do it diligently; if it is to show mercy, do it cheerfully."* [Ro.12:7-8]. To this indicative list of gifts, we can surely include celibacy: 'If *your* gift is celibacy, do it... *[add your adverb e.g. faithfully]*.' Every gift, whatever it is, is a God-grace and to be used in proportion to our faith; we can therefore reasonably expect harmony between gift-giver (God) and gift-receiver (us).

Having only ever been presented with the 'option' of celibacy, as if their God-given 'thorn in the flesh' [2Co.12:6-10], some appear reluctant to accept alternative options are available. Telling others, "We've had to *endure* this 'gift' so you should too", seems a less healthy approach.

Promoting the likes of True Freedom Trust and Living Out, and their carefully curated testimonies, enables some conservative evangelicals opposed to LGBTQ+ inclusion to claim they are not discriminatory towards gay brothers and sisters in Christ and, crucially, that even those who are gay support their conservative belief that sex can only be between a man and a woman in heterosexual marriage. I respect that some gay Christians have concluded that, *for them*, celibacy is the right path. Presented with the 'conservative' binary choice of being either gay or a disciple of Christ, they are choosing Christ. They are embracing the celibate life as both a call and gift, just as do some straight Christians. But life-long singleness is not the only option available to gay followers of Christ. Surely *true* freedom is having the liberty to be whole-heartedly the person God has wired you to be. Suppression of sexual orientation can have significant mental health consequences.

Back to church history. The 'new norm' of Christendom arguably led to a tamer, more state-controlled, societal version of faith. There's a lesson here for those campaigning for LGBTQ+ change today: be aware of what you lose when you become adopted by the mainstream. The price for adoption into more mainstream culture, as evidenced by the increasing media bandwidth and corporate sponsorship (airlines, banks, supermarkets, utilities...) of the Pride movement, is perhaps a tamer, sanitised expression of the radical Pride marches of the late 1970s and 80s that were originally made in response to the 1969 police raid on the Stonewall Inn in New York.

> ### To think about...
>
> 1. Are the 'majority' always right? When have you experienced a majority being wrong? A minority being right?
>
> 2. When it comes to sexuality, how are you being transformed by Christ in your thinking/ attitudes?

22

The Metanarrative

T hose who affirm LGBTQ+ inclusion and those who oppose it come together in recognising the need to tell the Bible's 'big story', from Genesis to Revelation – its meta-narrative. With 66 books, 1,189 chapters, and 32,003 verses, it's too easy to lose perspective.

A 'conservative/ traditionalist' metanarrative

Rev Dr Stephen Finamore, President of the Baptist Union of Great Britain (2024-2025) and former Principal of Bristol Baptist College, has done much to articulate the conservative meta-narrative and opposition to same-sex marriage. It's important to hear this perspective and so, with Stephen's gracious permission, I reproduce in full his succinct and well-argued objection to Ministers being in same-sex relationships (a debate currently being had in a number of Church traditions.)[98]

"While it is true that the Bible contains references to many different forms of marriage, the New Testament advocates only one. In particular, when He is asked about divorce, Jesus answers with a question about the Law, but then goes on to teach about marriage on the basis of how things were at the beginning [Mt.19:1-9 & Mk.10.2-9]. He refers explicitly to the creation of humanity as male and female and to the story of Adam and Eve, and cites the passage about a man leaving his parents and clinging to his wife with whom he becomes 'one flesh'. [Ge.1.27 & 2.24]. In other words, long before the giving of the Law, and before any act of primal human disobedience, the unity of a man and a woman in a relationship that Jesus understands as marriage, was a part of God's purposes in creation.

Elsewhere in the New Testament, Paul, an apostle, makes use of one of these passages in his teaching on sexual misconduct, strongly implying that, in his view, sexual activity belongs within heterosexual marriage. He argues that the Christian's body is not their own to do with as he or she may please, but belongs to God and is to be used for His glory [1Co.6:16-20].

Elsewhere, in discussing the mutual responsibilities involved in marriage, and again relying on Genesis 2.24, the letter to the Ephesians makes a link between Christians being members of Christ's body and the way that a man and a woman belong to one another in marriage. [Eph.5:28-33].

At the end of the Bible, in the book of Revelation, when the prophecy turns to visions of re-creation, one of the images used is that of a marriage supper [Rev.19:7-9]. One of the pictures for the union of God with His peoples, for the joining of heaven and earth, the great reconciliation of primal difference, is the union of a man and a woman in marriage [Rev.21:2-4].

The New Testament's theology of sex and marriage is undergirded by the writers' understanding of Genesis 1–2. They see the distinction between male and female as something primal and woven into the fabric of creation. The primal human, the Adam of Genesis 2, is divided so that male and female can both exist [Ge.2:21-22] and so that their union can be a sign of God's presence in creation and his purposes for it. The use of this idea in Ephesians demonstrates that this union of difference is a picture of Christ's unity with His Church. The use of marriage as an illustration in Revelation indicates that it functions as a picture of God's ultimate desire to be united with His peoples. In other words, heterosexual marriage, the union of persons whose difference is primal, is a good within creation, is a sign of the salvation that God offers in Christ and is a picture of the time when heaven and earth are one. It speaks of creation, salvation, and new creation. The difference between those involved is fundamental to the purpose.

One implication of this must be that whatever value there might or might not be in covenanted same-sex relationships, they cannot carry the same theological meaning as heterosexual marriage. They are not the same thing, and they should not be called by the same name by the Church, even if the State chooses to do so.

A second implication is surely that God has offered us two ways to be human adults. We can be single, or we can be married to a person of the opposite sex.

Those called to ministry among us are called to be exemplary disciples. They recognize that God's calling on their lives is the thing that defines their being and their purpose. All other parts of their being are secondary and are subject to their identity in Christ. If they are to reflect God and his purposes for creation, not just in what they do but in who they are, they will either be single or will be a partner in a heterosexual marriage. It is therefore appropriate for the Baptist Union ministerial guidelines to regard sexual relationships between people of the same sex, and indeed all sexual relationships other than heterosexual marriage, as conduct unbecoming of those called to be ministers and to therefore constitute gross misconduct for the purposes of the ministerial guidelines."

Rev Dr Stephen Finamore   May 2022

> *To think about...*
>
>   1. Why is it important to tell the Bible's metanarrative?
>
>   2. What do you find helpful about Steve Finamore's summary?
>
>   3. What, if anything, would you add, amend, or omit from it?

I'm grateful to Rev Dr Finamore for giving voice to those who read and love the same Bible and yet have a different perspective to me. I agree with much of it! My issue is not so much what this statement says, rather what it omits. Is the 'big picture' really that heterosexual God created a heterosexual world in which only heterosexual people can flourish? If so, it sounds like another form of 'limited atonement'.[99] Surely the story of God, and the metanarrative of the Bible, is much bigger than this? For balance, I offer an alternative: a metanarrative to inclusion *and beyond*. Lacking the sharpness of Steve Finamore's mind, and wanting to highlight aspects that others sometimes omit, my attempt is longer.

An inclusive and beyond metanarrative

NT Wright proposes a 'five act' hermeneutic, grouping the Bible into five progressive stages: Creation; Fall; Israel; Jesus; Church.[100] He acknowledges 'other models exist', and that the final scenes of the New Testament, as described in Revelation, look suspiciously like the start of a new 'act', if not a new play altogether. For this reason, I will add a sixth act: Heaven. As Alpha and Omega, Christ is there before *Act One: Creation* begins, and is there at The End of *Act Six: Heaven (The End!)*. The story in between is of God's redemptive plan to recreate us.

Act 1: Creation

"In the beginning, God..." [Ge.1:1] Before *anything*, God was *everything*. There was nothing else but God: Eternal, without equal or comparison, who was, is, and is to come – Almighty [Rev.1:8]. Though perfectly and completely One [Dt.6:4], triune-God, Father, Son and Holy Spirit, exists as Divine Spirit and Personality. Community, relationships, plurality, even difference/ diversity, are at the heart of God; hence, *"Let us.. in our image.."* [Ge.1:26]. God's better pronouns are [they/them]; singular, yet also plural.

...*"God created the heavens and the earth."* [Ge.1:1], and everything else, declaring it all 'good'. Just as a masterpiece reveals the character of the artist, so Creation reveals God's beauty, creativity, power, diversity... There aren't just bees; there are over 20,000 different kinds of bees (we keep discovering more!) Just as well that there are 400,000 different types of flowers, with 20,000 varieties of daisies! God is truly omni-creative. Diversity, biodiversity, is both good and core to Creation.

Being Divine Relationship, God made humanity (adam, man/mankind) in *their* [God's] image [Ge.1:26] and declared us *very* good. Every individual without exception, whether gay or straight, has infinite worth as God's handiwork, priceless treasure [Eph.2:10]. Likewise, we are all born pre-loaded with a spiritual capacity for God, carrying the 'divine spark', the breath of God [Ge.2:7].

There was a time when 'adam' was humanity – everyone. Paul says 'adam' is representative of all of us [1Co.15:22]. Just as the 'first Adam' represented all humanity, so we are all represented by the 'last Adam', Christ [1Co.15:45]. No-one claims, because incarnate Jesus was male, therefore Christ is only representative of men[101]. Therefore, 'Genesis Adam' is black, brown, white, female, male, non-binary, lesbian, gay, bi, trans, queer, straight... Adam is all of us, whoever we are, however we identify.

Just as God is One and yet also plural (us/our), so humanity is both singular (mankind/ humanity) and yet also plural (male and female). We shouldn't be too binary about this. The One who we are made through, will later declare, *"There is neither Jew nor Gentile, neither slave nor free, nor is there male and female, for you are all one in Christ Jesus"* [Gal. 3:28]. Instead, there is plurality, difference, even fluidity, from the start. Poignantly, Genesis does not pitch a binary male _or_ female, one or the other; rather male _and_ female. Whilst Genesis poetically talks of 'day and night', 'land and sea', 'man and woman', God creates a non-binary reality that is far more fluid. Light and dark are a spectrum, with degrees of dawn and dusk (at any one moment with each part of the world seeing it differently.) If where 'land' ends and 'sea' begins is graduated by tides, beaches, marshes, reedbeds, and swamp, then why can't 'male' and 'female' also be a spectrum? We don't expect all future couples to mirror the first couple – the only two people at that time to exist on Earth – in *their* age, ethnicity, or other characteristic, so why do we expect all to replicate their heterosexuality? Whatever the gender identity, all are equally made in, and so collectively reflect, the image of God.

Wanting us to experience what God enjoys, 'Adam' was given the gift of relationship, a co-helping equal 'soul mate' in 'Eve'. We get a more complete image of God with a plurality and diversity of people. God blessed and commanded humanity to 'be fruitful and increase in number' [Ge. 1:27]. Creation is sustained through procreation. Sex is part of the divine plan, made pleasurable as an incentive (not just a biological function). And with _no_ shame.

All this is pure Shalom – God-created completeness, equilibrium, wholeness – between God and Creation, between people, across the genders, within each individual, and with humanity and the rest of Creation. This Eden is Heaven on Earth! No wonder God is pleased with the beautiful, diverse and relational world He has made. It is _very good!_

To think about...

.. that word VERY. God declared all humanity VERY good.

Act 2: Fall

What began as the ultimate idyll, Heaven on Earth, with diverse humanity at perfect peace (Shalom) with God, one another, and the rest of creation, was shattered by strife and disunity.

In 'Adam', all humanity succumbed to alternative 'glass half empty' narratives that misrepresented God as restrictive, harsh, distant, and withholding. We still do. Scientists at Yale have used satellite imagery and ground survey data to conclude there are now three trillion trees on Earth .[102] What's more, 12,000 years ago (before agriculture took off) there were twice as many. That's 6,000,000,000,000 or six million millions. That's a lot of trees! And God said, you can eat from all of them, except just *one*. That doesn't sound too limiting.

We blamed God, everyone and everything for our own actions. We still do. The equality and mutuality between people gave way to gender wars: blaming, labelling (naming), shaming. All expressions of oppression – patriarchy, sexism, racism, homophobia – find their source here.

Whilst God intended that no shame be associated with sex, nakedness, or our human bodies [Ge.2:25], the Fall changed all that. As a result of sin, sex was tainted by power and coercive control, even leading to: violence and murder [Ge.4:1-12]; incest [Ge.4:17]; polygamy [Ge.4:19]; sexual exploitation [Ge.6:1-5]; indecency [Ge.9:20-25]; rape [Ge.34:1-7]. Pregnancy, a consequence of sex, was rendered painful [Ge.3:16]. Some argue Genesis 3 establishes a heterosexual 'husband and wife', where the woman dotes subserviently and the man rules [Ge.3:16], but of course this is in the context of the Fall where nothing is quite as it should be.

The Fall was not just a one-off event. Even in Genesis there are numerous 'falls': Adam and Eve [Ge.3]; Cain and Abel [Ge.4]; the Sethites [Ge.5:1-8]. If we're honest, we all know what it is to 'fall,' and have been affected by other people's 'falls'. We experience the pain of chaos. Adam and Eve is *our* story. However we identify, whatever our sexuality, *"all have sinned and fall short of the glory of God"* [Ro.3:23] None of us live up to our own standards, let alone to God's. Today, we use strong and secure WiFi passwords with their string of upper and lower-case letters, numbers, and characters. Whether we are just one digit off or wide of the mark is immaterial; access is denied. Grading some 'sins' and 'sinners' better or worse than others is a very human, judgmental habit, but utterly pointless.

If the wages (consequences) of sin is death [Ro.6:23], it's like suggesting corpses argue who's more dead. Even if, for argument's sake, a faithful and consenting same-sex relationship was 'sin' (which, by now, it's clear I don't believe), it's no more sinful than a straight couple's faithful and consenting marriage. So, why target lesbian, gay, bi, trans or queer people? Jesus wryly said, *"Why do you look at the speck of sawdust in your brother's eye and pay no attention to the plank in your own eye?"* [Mt.7:3-5]. With God, all means ALL have sinned, whatever our age, ethnicity, gender, neuropathway, sexuality...

Luke says, *"Forgive us our sin"* (not *sins*) [Lk.11:4]. Sin is not so much a list of broken rules and regulations; it's far more a broken relationship, being out of connection with God; the absence of Shalom. A state of sin separates us from God and each other, leaving us feeling broken, fallen, separated from God.

Yet, immediately there was a plan to reconcile humanity back into right relationship with God, everyone, and everything – to restore Shalom: *"The Lord God made garments of skin for Adam and his wife and clothed them"* [Ge.3:21]. Instead of heaping even more shame on to us, God will lift our shame. How? Through sacrifice: Jesus' atoning sacrifice on the Cross. Jesus doesn't just save us from the effects of death and sin, but also from all the other consequences of 'the Fall': judging others and being judged; oppressing others and being oppressed; shaming others and being shamed; even from our racism, sexism, and, yes, our homophobia too.

> ### To think about...
> What happens when sex is associated with sin and shame?

Act 3: Israel

Not giving up on humanity, God seeks to woo and restore us into healthy relationship, even if that requires a patient long game. Just as populating Earth starts with one, then two, so God then looks for 'some' and calls them Israel.

God's vision was never just for *some*; it was always for ALL – to inclusion *and beyond*. God's intent was that *"ALL people on earth will be blessed"* through Abram and his descendants. [Ge.12:3]. These will number more than there are stars in the Heavens [Ge.15:5] or grains of sand on the Earth [Ge.22:17]. Researchers at the University of Hawaii guesstimate there are 7.5×10^{18} grains of sand, or seven quintillion, five hundred quadrillion. Others suggest it's more like five sextillion grains of sand. That's 5 billion billion, or a '5' with 21 zeros. Whatever, that's a lot of sand; yet there are even more stars. There are said to be 70 thousand million, million, million stars in the observable universe. Just in our galaxy, the Milky Way, there are 100 to 400 billion stars, and there are more than 100 billion galaxies in the Universe – maybe as many as 500 billion. If you multiply stars by galaxies, even at the low end, you get ten billion billion stars, or ten sextillion stars in the Universe – a '1' followed by 22 zeros. Some put it as high as 100 sextillion stars.

Population experts think 115 billion people have lived on Earth to date. That's a lot of people but nothing compared to the number of stars or grains of sand. Once again, in a pre-scientific age, Genesis is using hyperbole (code for "a lot") to speak a bigger truth: God is on a mission to inclusion *and beyond*. Whilst 'some' is better than than two (Adam & Eve), what God truly desires is ALL people.

Incidentally, Abram was married to Sarai [Ge.11:29], his half-sister, a blood relative [Ge.20:11-13]. Whatever constituted their marriage was evidently very different to our understanding today. We expect a state-recognised marriage ceremony, evidenced by a marriage certificate and an Instagram photoshoot. Abram and Sarai were 'married' in that they were living together in a committed relationship.

Israel is not just a nation, but a *people* [De.7:6], holy and pleasing to God, not because of who they are and what they have done, but because of God and what He has done [De.9:4-6]. They are to model God's justice in their inclusion of everyone [De.10:17-18; 24:17; 27:19]. Hospitality and non-judgmental welcome were not just of people 'like us'; even 'eunuchs', condemned in the Mosaic Law for having had their testicles removed [De.23:1], were to be welcomed. Yahweh was on a mission to inclusion *and beyond*, gathering those 'othered' and excluded, and including them too in Zion [Isa.56:6-8].

Unsurprisingly, the archetypal Patriarchs (Abraham, Isaac, Jacob, Joseph, Moses, Joshua, David…) mostly used male pronouns for Israel [Ex.2:22; Je.31:10; Hos.11:1], even though it comprised women as well as men. Yet, at other times, Israel was given female pronouns [Jer.3:6-8; Hos.2:1-23]. Israel is 'daughter Israel, the bride of Yahweh' [Isa.54:5-8 ; Jer.31:31-34], as well as an unfaithful female prostitute [Jer.3:1] or a pregnant woman [Rev.12]; other times, Israel is God's firstborn son [Ex.4:22-23]. There is gender fluidity within Israel. Given that (male) Bible writers presumptuously gave God male pronouns, the marriage between God and Israel can be considered either an opposite-sex or same-sex union. Of course, the gender or sexual orientation of the 'bride' wasn't the point; so those who can't yet affirm LGBTQ+ relationships would be wise not to make it that.

Then, in one of those chapters in the Bible you think, *'what the heck?'*, Ezekiel chapter sixteen uncomfortably portrays Israel as a naked pubescent girl whom God, seeing she now has grown breasts and pubic hair and so is finally 'old enough for love', then entered into a 'covenant' with her and 'took' her as His own [v.6-8]. No euphemisms required. However, Israel then became a prostitute, "spreading her legs with increasing promiscuity to anyone who passed by" [v.25], including those with 'large genitals' [v.26]. "You adulterous wife! You prefer strangers to your own husband!"

So into 'the scene', Israel was giving free 'gifts' to all her lovers [v.31]. Then, if that was not enough, it says, as her punishment, God will orchestrate her gang rape and violent death [v.35-42]. And then, of course, Sodom is brought up; only, once again, it's nothing to do with sexual orientation:

> **"Now THIS was the sin of your sister Sodom: she and her daughters were arrogant, overfed and unconcerned; they did not help the poor and needy. They were haughty and did detestable things before me."**
> *Ezekiel 16:49-50*

As hurt and angry as God was with Israel, He still seeks ~~her him~~ *them*, <u>us</u>, back. Most 'conservatives' rightly recognise this as a metaphor. Yet, we shouldn't overlook the rawness of the text and, if we accept this is metaphor, why not other passages too? God says, despite everything, *"Yet I will remember the covenant I made with you"* [Ez.16:60]. Covenant is a recurring theme, connecting Genesis to Revelation, in which God commits to bringing about His good purpose in individuals and <u>all</u> humanity. Covenant was first beautifully symbolised by the rainbow [Gen.9:8-17] – no longer were those beautifully made in God's image to be subjected to sacrilegious violence. Covenants are normally made by two parties. For example, in England, when 'buyer' and 'seller' agree a property sale, they enter into a covenant, a legally binding promise to 'exchange'. Instead, God issues a one-sided Covenant. He wasn't imposing severe terms or conditions on Noah; if you do X, I'll do Y. Instead, He was making a unilateral Covenant promise to bless all people. No wonder rainbows are the 'go to' symbol for peace (Shalom) and inclusion.

Prophet Joel brings together many of the themes of the Old Testament – exodus, Law, exile, judgment, and hope – and points to the 'Day of the Lord' that is still to come. To beleaguered Israel with its 'glass half empty' view of God, he says, *"Rend your heart, not your garments. Return to the*

Lord your God, for He is gracious and compassionate, slow to anger and abounding in love" [Joel 2:13]. Joel could see a time coming when this would be for <u>all</u> people, not just for some, regardless of age, class, culture, ethnicity, gender, or any other human-construct label.

> **"I will pour out my Spirit on <u>all</u> people. Your sons and daughters will prophesy, your old men will dream dreams, your young men will see visions. Even on my servants, both men and women, I will pour out my Spirit in those days... And <u>everyone</u> who calls on the name of the Lord will be saved..."**   *Joel 2:28-32*

'Act Three: Israel' anticipates and prepares the way for *'Act Four: Jesus'*.

> **To think about...**
> Jesus summarised the Law as 'love God, love others, love yourself. Is that how you see it?

Act 4: Jesus

If you want to know what God is like, look at Jesus. He is the image of the invisible God [Col.1:15], the Original we are all copied from. That means, all that Jesus was, is, and is to come is totally relevant to the question of inclusion *and beyond*. We interpret the whole of Scripture through the revelation of Christ; the Word of God understood through Logos, <u>*The*</u> Word of God. Any attempt to explain, or explain away, inclusion that isn't immersed in the words, works, and wonders of Jesus is no Gospel.

As 'Alpha', Jesus was there 'In the beginning [Ge.1:1; Jn.1-1]; as 'Omega', He will be there at the completion of all things. He's from everlasting, to everlasting; from eternity, to all eternity. He is the trajectory that we all find ourselves on.

So significant is Jesus, when He was born, the whole world said, 'stop the clock, re-set the calendar'. We now date everything according to whether it's BC or AD, Before Christ or Anno Domini (in the year of the Lord). Yet, Jesus was born on the margins: in an outpost of the oppressive Roman Empire, on the Continent of Asia, in the Middle East – not in Rome, or even Jerusalem, but a small town with a powerful connection to King David. God was making a point. The one who lifts our shame [Ro.10:1 1-13] was born out of 'wedlock' to an unmarried teenage girl; so shamed and shunned by her partner's 'religious elite' family, despite the all-important 'hospitality code', the young couple were left alone for the birth of their first child, in a 'Levitically' unclean cowshed, surrounded by unclean animals. Incarnate Christ came, not to endorse exclusion, but overcome it.

Christ's birth was announced, not to the 'great and good', but to shepherds labelled 'unclean'[103] and to mystic Magi from modern-day Iraq. Angels proclaimed good news for <u>all</u> people [Lk.2:10] and sung, *"Glory to God in the highest heaven, and on earth peace [Shalom] to those on whom his favour rests."* [Lk.2:14]. Though we often prefer to sing of Christ's majesty and power, there was a time when God Incarnate was a 'helpless babe' 'wrapped in cloths' [Lk.2:12], unable to roll over, feed Himself or even control His bowel movements. We should be wary of religion that seeks power and control. This Jesus, at the end of His radical life, will again be washed, prepared and wrapped in strips of cloth. But by then not even those strips could contain Him.

With His selection of twelve disciples, mirroring the twelve tribes of Israel, Jesus was demonstrating He was the *new* Israel. He was on a mission, fulfilling what Israel had been called to be but had never become [Isa.61: 1-2] – for all:

"The Spirit of the Lord is on me, because he has anointed me to proclaim good news to the poor. He has sent me to proclaim freedom for the prisoners and recovery of

sight for the blind, to set the oppressed free, to proclaim the year of the Lord's favour." Luke 4:18-19

Jesus was applying Scripture in ways that didn't fit traditionalists' meta-narrative; hence why He called out their populist soundbites which they had always been given to believe were in the Bible but, it transpires, weren't [Lk.4:23][104], and resisted their attempts to dictate His mission. Furious, these otherwise deeply religious people sought to kill off this inclusive incarnation of the Messiah. Why the strong, visceral reaction? After all, Jesus wasn't telling anyone they were no longer included, rather that *everyone* was included. What's so bad about that?

The poor are not just those without money: they're everyone who's ever felt 'spent', with nothing left to give (physically, psychologically, emotionally, socially, spiritually); beaten up by life, even by religion [Mt.11:28-30]. For those who feel at the end of their rope or grieve for those that lost their fight; feel put down by the powerful or are exhausted by the long struggle for inclusion; respond to crass judgement with grace... good news! Jesus declared, be blessed, God is on your side."You're blessed when you're at the end of your rope. With less of you there is more of God and his rule. As Eugene Peterson beautifully put it:

> **"You're blessed when you feel you've lost what is most dear to you. Only then can you be embraced by the One most dear to you. You're blessed when you're content with just who you are—no more, no less. That's the moment you find yourselves proud owners of everything that can't be bought. You're blessed when you've worked up a good appetite for God. He's food and drink in the best meal you'll ever eat. You're blessed when you care. At the moment of being 'care-full,' you find yourselves cared for. You're blessed when you get your inside**

world—your mind and heart—put right. Then you can see God in the outside world. You're blessed when you can show people how to cooperate instead of compete or fight. That's when you discover who you really are, and your place in God's family. You're blessed when your commitment to God provokes persecution. The persecution drives you even deeper into God's kingdom. Not only that—count yourselves blessed every time people put you down or throw you out or speak lies about you to discredit me. What it means is that the truth is too close for comfort and they are uncomfortable. You can be glad when that happens—give a cheer, even!—for though they don't like it, I do! And all heaven applauds. And know that you are in good company. My prophets and witnesses have always gotten into this kind of trou ble." Matthew 5:3-12, The Message

Jesus is good news for those the 'religious elite', with their 'glass half empty' view of God, judged unacceptable: women [Mk.5:25-34]; those too young [Mt.19:13-15] or too old [Mk.1:29-31; Lk.7:11-17]; the sick [Lk.8:1-4]; those born with a disability [Lk.5:17-26] or long-term chronic conditions [Lk.13:10-17]; Gentiles [Mt.8:5-13; 15:21-18; Jn.4:1-26] ; those judged for being too political [Mk.3:18] or colluding 'with the world' [Lk.5:27-32]; those whose 'relationship status' is 'complicated' [Jn.4:1-26]; and those simply labelled 'sinners'. Jesus modelled this by frequently socialising with 'sinners', thus – unlike those in Sodom and Gomorrah, and much to the 'religious elites' annoyance – living by the 'hospitality code' [Mt.10:14-15]. Jesus was, still is, good news for _all_, whatever age, ethnicity, gender, neuropathway, physical ability, or sexuality.

Instead, it was the self-righteous 'religious elite' that Jesus consistently 'called out' [Mk.2;17]. It's not those who claim they're healthy that need a doctor, it's the sick – 'the rest of us' [Lk.5:31-32]. Jesus couldn't have been any clearer: *"Do not judge, or you too will be judged"* [Mt.7:1-2]; do not obsess with the speck in your sibling's eye, when your own perspective is so compromised by the log in your own eye [Mt.7:3-5]. They were hypocrites *who "shut the door of the kingdom of heaven in people's faces"*, fixating on isolated Levitical pixels but failing to grasp God's bigger picture: justice, mercy and faithfulness [Mt.23:13-39].

Jesus told a story about someone 'on a journey' from Jerusalem to Jericho [Lk.10:25-37], a distance of only 20 miles but through lawless Samaria. Most circumnavigated to avoid 'going there', but not this one. Alas, robbers used intimidation and violence to attack his humanity, leaving him battered, half-dead, half-alive. A 'hate crime'. In the traditional version of this populist tale, the 'baddies' were always Samaritans (because they had integrated with Gentiles) and the 'goodies' Jewish (because they upheld the Law). But this is Jesus. In His version, neither the Priest nor Levite showed any compassion, even to 'one of their own'. Their preoccupation with, and narrow interpretation of, a few pixels of the Law [Lev.21:1; Nu.19:11], whilst failing to grasp its bigger picture – love God, love others, love yourself – meant they would rather let the traveller die than risk being contaminated, and so lose possible future ministry opportunities. They wouldn't even engage; they 'passed by on the *other* side'. Instead, it was a much-maligned Samaritan who put aside prejudice to offer acceptance, hospitality, and healing, going the 'extra mile for his 'sibling'. Jesus poignantly asked the expert in the Law, and now us, *'Which of these showed true love to their neighbour?'* Whilst a 'conservative/ traditionalist congregation might be surprised to discover their Samaritan is gay, an affirming church might equally be blindsided if theirs turned out to be a 'conservative/ traditionalist'. The point is, love sees beyond centuries-old prejudices and modern-day 'position statements' to love 'others' as God loves them, whatever their identity. Being secure enough to do this, is a sign of healthy self-love.

A woman was dragged into the Temple and accused of adultery [Jn.7:5 3-8:11]. Even though everyone knows adultery takes two, only the *woman* was publicly humiliated and shamed – so already, in this toxic religious setting, the Law was being selectively applied to privilege some and condemn others. The different experiences of 'straight' and queer Christians today would suggest it's still happening. It's *possible* this woman had been raped. In language highly uncomfortable today, Deuteronomy 22 portrays women as 'property', first of their father, then of their husband. Those that are raped in the city are said to be adulterous and stoned to death, along with their rapist [De.22:23-24]. Imagine someone is racially abused, and *they* are sent to prison, along with their racist attacker. The 'religious elite' must have known what Jesus' inclusive stance would be; they were curating Scripture to reflect their own values. It was a trap.

With poignant silence, Jesus wrote something in the dirt that only they know to this day, before eventually saying, *"Let any one of you who is without sin be the first to throw a stone at her."* [Jn.7:53-8:11]. Jesus wasn't condemning her; He was calling out the hypocrisy of her religioaccusers. No longer did she have to defend herself. As NT Wright observes, they began wanting to stone the woman to death, but ended wanting to stone Jesus.[105] Of course, the "Yes, buts" are always quick to say, yes but, Jesus told her to leave her life of sin. True, but Jesus was making the point, her accusers – with their use of shame, weaponizing of selective Scriptures, and hypocrisy – were as much 'sinners'. If she had been raped, surely the point was, you no longer need live with this accusation. In this story, we are all this woman; what we must not be is the 'religious elite'. Frequently, Jesus says, "You have heard it said... But *I tell you*..." He wasn't replacing or contradicting the Law, He was fulfilling its true purpose, correcting the 'religious elite's' distorted caricature.

Alas, even the disciples who prided themselves on being closest to Christ sought to stop others they deemed on the margins of orthodoxy. Jesus rebuked them too: *"Whoever is not against you, is for you"* [Lk.9:49-50]. Why invest energy attacking sibling believers, when the mission before us is so challenging? Will opposing LGBTQ+ inclusion lead to more or fewer people following Christ? Where is the evidence of fruit [Mt.7:15-20], and will it outlast the strategic mission funding, when the myriad salaried posts have all gone? Jesus does not privilege the majority; He leaves the ninety-nine to go after the one [Lk.15:1-7] for they too carry the image of the Divine [Mt.18:15].

What is beyond doubt, Jesus taught and modelled love. Remember, when asked by that expert in the Law, Jesus summarised the Old Testament as *"Love God, love others, love yourself"* [Lk.10:27]. Later, Paul affirmed, *"For the entire law is fulfilled in keeping this one command: 'Love your neighbour as yourself"* [Gal.5:14]. That everything should be filtered through love is not surprising given that God IS love [1Jn.4:7-8]. Just as God is not just good and perfect Father but the source of all fatherhood from which all human fathers are mere copies[106] [Eph.3:14-21], so God is not just loving, but the source of all Love. If you have ever loved something or someone, or been loved by someone, you've had a Divine experience because God IS Love. Everything God is, and everything that God does, is because of Love.

If we are made in the image of God and, in Christ, enabled to 'participate in the divine nature' [2Pet.1:3-4], and if the essence of God IS love, then humanity is made in the image of love. This applies to ALL people, whether male or female, young or old, gay, lesbian, bi, trans, queer, or straight, whatever our ethnicity, heritage, or other label.

It is because God is love that He *"so loved the world that whoever [no asterisked small print exclusions apply] believes in Him shall not perish but have eternal life"* [Jn.3:16]. Jesus was emphatic: He had not come to condemn, rather to save; the only criterion being belief in Christ [Jn.3:17] – nothing ese.

Some 'conservatives/ traditionalists' dismiss this focus on love as 'wishy-washy' sentimentalism. Where is the emphasis on sin and righteousness, they ask? Again, it's a "yes, but" response. Any portrayal of Scripture that does not take seriously the essence of God, as revealed in Christ, the Word of God, is profoundly flawed. It is *this* Jesus who is *the* Way, *the* Truth, and *the* Life. No one – not even 'conservatives/ traditionalists' come to the Father except through Christ [Jn.14:6] – as He is revealed in Scripture.

This love was magnified on the Cross. *"Greater love has no one than this: to lay down one's life for one's friends"* [Jn.15:13]. Whilst intellectually I know that some theologically Reformed Christians believe in 'limited atonement' (the belief that, in effect, Jesus only died for those God pre-selected to believe in Him – not for everyone), I struggle to reconcile this with Scripture's 'big picture'. God so loved the *world*, not just the 'straight' ones [Jn.3:16]; Jesus died for sin once *and for <u>all</u>* [1Pe.3:18]. On the Cross, Jesus carried our sin and lifted our shame. It's a total 'game changer' that gives us all a new 'in Christ' super-identity that trumps (but, crucially, does not replace) all other human labels and protected characteristics.

> *"From now on we regard no one from a worldly point of view. Though we once regarded Christ in this way, we do so no longer. Therefore, if anyone is in Christ, the new creation has come: the old has gone, the new is here! All this is from God, who reconciled us to himself through Christ and gave us the ministry of reconciliation."* 2 Corinthians 5:16-18

Of course, a radical life that ends with a sacrificial death, may be inspirational, but then so too were Mohandas Gandhi, Dr Martin Luther King, Jr., and Mother Theresa. They lived and died. Jesus is unique: He died and lived. The one who said He'd come to give us life, and life in all its abundance (widescreen, vivid colour) [Jn.10:10], is the Author of Life itself – the source of all life and love. Christianity without the resurrection of Jesus is merely a collection of moral stories, self-help teachings, and a nice way to meet people on a Sunday. The resurrection was the ultimate

Divine vindication of all that Christ was, said, and did. Because He lives, not only can we face tomorrow, we must also take seriously what He said about living today.

Having previously told the Twelve to go only to the 'lost sheep of Israel' (the *'some'*) [Mt.10:5-6], *'Act Four: Jesus'* closes with Christ's great commission to go to *all:*

> *"Therefore, go and make disciples of all <u>nations</u>, baptising them in the name of the Father and of the Son and of the Holy Spirit, and teaching them to obey everything <u>I have commanded</u> you. And surely I am with you always, to the very end of the age.'"*
> Matthew 28:18-20

'All nations' is better understood as all peoples, sub-cultures, identities. This includes LGBTQ+ communities, with myriad expressions. The call for *'Act Five: Church'* is to continue Christ's trajectory – His mission and ministry – to the 'ends of the earth' [Ac.1:8]; extending God's radically inclusive Kingdom to all, not inculcating our own conditioned prejudices and flawed agendas [Mt.24:24]. Jesus was, and – if authentically represented – still is, truly good news. That means He is good news for those who are lesbian, gay, bi, trans, queer, or straight.

To think about...
WWJD – what would Jesus do?

Act 5: Church

Fifty days after that holiest of weeks, culminating in the death and resurrection of Christ, Jerusalem was once again full of people from all corners of their 'known world'. They had come for the Jewish Festival of Shavuot, celebrating harvest and the gift of the Law. Then the Spirit of Christ came. Suddenly, because of '*Act Four: Jesus*', the 'some' of '*Act Three: Israel*' became part of the 'all' of '*Act Five: Church*'. It was as if the Tower of Babel [Ge.11:1-9], with its divisive language, cultural barriers, and human-construct borders, was being replaced by a growing community of people from every nation; the peoples, sub-cultures, and identities that Jesus had commissioned His followers to reach out to and include in God's Kingdom. The Church was born to be inclusive; not surprising, given it's the body of Christ [Ro.12:5; 1Cor.12:12-27], with Jesus as its Head [2Cor.11:12; Eph.5:23; Col.1:18].

Just as the human body is built on unity in diversity, so is Christ's body, the Church. Uniformity without diversity – say, just hands, no other body parts – is usually a crime scene, an indicator of violence. Paul says our unity is found in Jesus, not in our myriad human-construct labels, be that ethnicity, gender, socio-economic status (or, we might add, neuropathway, physical ability, sexuality..) [1Co.12:13]. Churches with a mix of lesbian, gay, bi, trans, queer, and straight people have a richer experience of what it means to be the body of Christ, than those who curate 'people like us'. Paul goes further: we are to privilege those members of the body that we were previously conditioned to think of less favourably [1Co.12:23]. With a history of exclusion, it's now appropriate to give special honour to LGBTQ+ siblings in Christ.

Like Israel, the Church was ascribed gender fluidity. As the *Body* of Christ, it is presumed male (despite it also comprising women) and described in ways perceived *at that time* as masculine: it is the 'army of God' [Ph.2:25; Phil.1:2; Rev.19:14], whose soldiers wear armour [Eph.6:11-17]; its pastors were 'shepherds of the flock'. Yet, as the *Bride* of Christ it has often been gendered female (despite also comprising men). Other times, gender-neutral terms were used, like branches of a vine [Jn.15:5-8]; a mixed-gender family [Mt.12:48-50; 2Cor.6:18]; the house of God [1Co.3:16-17; 1Ti.3:14-15; 1Pe.2:5]. If the 'Christ as Groom/ Bride of Christ' metaphor is used to legislate marriage between two individuals, then it could be said to support same-sex marriage as equally as heterosexual marriage.

The Church was never meant to be just a patched-up Israel [Lk.5:36-39], more effective at accommodating 'some'. Too often, like the Pharisee who declared, *"God, I thank you that I am not like other people – robbers, evildoers, adulterers – or even like this tax collector"* [Lk.18:11], we have defined who's 'in' by who we've kept 'out'. Instead, we are called to continue the mission and ministry of Christ, surpassing in reach and scale [Jn.14:12]. Even incarnate Jesus, bound by very human limitations of time and location, could only include, heal, and restore *some* – if He was 'there, then', He couldn't simultaneously be 'here, now' [Jn.11:1-44]. Yet, Resurrected Jesus, the Spirit of Christ, exercised through the Body of Christ, seeks to include, heal, and restore *all*. Religion that God accepts as pure and faultless goes to inclusion and beyond with those often excluded or overlooked [Jas.1:27].

A key task of the Church is to bring more of Heaven on Earth, to be the answer to our own prayer: *"Your Kingdom come, Your will be done, on Earth as it is in Heaven."* Heaven is not just where 'people like us' go to escape this rotten world when we die. By faith, we are to labour with Christ on His trajectory, bringing Heaven's justice, peace, and joy to Earth[107]; seeing Creation renewed and restored, in anticipation of the new Heaven and Earth. As God's domain, it reflects the Divine character, diversity and relationship of the Three-in: all that God is, likes, and does. It's what life looks like when Christ's "all nations" mission is completed [Mt:28:18-20] and His "that they be one" prayer answered [Jn.17:20-23]. Whatever Heaven is, it is surely vibrant, diverse, eclectic, surprising, and utterly joyful; true Shalom, the epicentre of Love. Through our faith and zeal, we are called to bring this about, right here, right now. That places a profound responsibility on the Church to both be and bring God's version of 'good news' to – and with – all.

The newborn Church was on Christ's trajectory, moving from an exclusive, monocultural sect within Judaism, led by men from Galilee in

Israel, to an inclusive and open multicultural community of people from 'every nation under heaven' [Ac.2:5]: Gentiles as well as Jews; Africans, Asians, and Europeans, not just Israelis; led by women as well as men. This trajectory led Paul to celebrate, *"The gospel is bearing fruit and growing throughout the whole world – just as it has been doing among you since the day you heard it and truly understood God's grace"* [Col.1:6]. Christ's trajectory is on-going, taking the gospel (radical good news) of the Kingdom to all people and places Paul didn't even know existed. *'Act Six: Heaven (The End!)'* is paused, waiting for us to fulfil this mission [Mt.24:14].

For all the talk of things only getting worse, we also see evidence of Kingdom values being progressively restored. It would be an indictment against the Church and Society if we didn't! Though the trajectory towards the liberation of women from oppressive patriarchy and misogyny is far from complete, positively, the feminist and womanist struggles of the last hundred years means *'Act Six: Heaven (The End!)'* is nearer than it once was. For example, in the UK, The Married Women's Property Acts (1870), The Parliamentary Qualification of Women Act (1918), Equal Franchise Act (1928), Equal Pay Act (1970), Sex Discrimination Act (1975), The Sexual Offences Act (2003), and The Equality Act (2010) all contribute in part towards realising that heavenly vision of justice and the love of God [Lk.11:42]. As Christ's trajectory progresses towards Completion, and we see more glimpses of Heaven on Earth, the Church, in many ways, is becoming more inclusive now than it's ever been. That's good news!

We all wear different and multiple labels; some we choose, others are projected onto us. These stem from the likes of our biology, geography, upbringing, culture, and social norms. Hopefully, we all come to appreciate *others* and our *self*. What unites us is our shared humanity. Yet, Paul goes further. When we become a follower of Jesus, we are given a new 'super label' that identifies us as being 'in Christ'; hence why Paul declares,

"There is neither Jew nor Greek, slave nor free, male nor female, for you are all one in Christ Jesus." Galatians 3:28

Boom. There it is. The new humanity!

It's not that we are to become blind to ethnicity, socio-economic status, gender, or other identity labels, but 'in Christ', there is no place for such hierarchies, divisions, or oppression. This list is clearly *indicative*, not exhaustive[108], of the myriad labels we humans create. It's not that those who carry these three specific identities that Paul cites are 'one in Christ', but all others remain excluded; <u>ALL</u> are one in Christ, including, whether lesbian, gay, bi, trans, queer, or straight. This was always God's plan because, as Paul, says, *"If you belong to Christ, then you are Abraham's seed, and heirs according to the promise."* [Gal.3:29] What Abraham and Sarah had hinted at – despite the stain of patriarchy, slavery, violence, and coercive control – is now being fulfilled in Christ through His body, the Church.

'Conservatives' and 'progressives' alike agree that Christ has removed the barriers to faith – all can be 'saved', whoever. For feminists and womanists, this also challenges the sin of gender inequality and the unequal experience of men and women, both in society and the Church. Many who can't yet affirm LGBTQ+ inclusion nevertheless accept the inclusion of women and their calling to ministry (though some 'conservatives/ traditionalists' still won't.)

The "Yes buts" say, this confirms a binary gender of either 'male' or 'female', with no other self-identifications available. Except, of course, there is fluidity within the other examples: there are shades of being Jewish (Orthodox, religious, traditional, secular..), and degrees of freedom and enslavement. What's more, Paul uses 'male' (arsen) and 'female' (thēly), not the everyday language of 'man' (aner) and 'woman' (gynē), as a nod to the Creation narrative [Ge 1:27]. Christ has inaugurated the new Creation, establishing God's Kingdom, Heaven on Earth. Whatever human distinctions we make for ourselves, we are all one 'in Christ'. In Jesus we gain not just a Saviour but also a spiritual family. It's unity over uniformity.

Through believer's baptism (or confirmation), we locate our story in Christ's story: His death, becomes our 'death', so that His resurrection becomes ours too. As we declare 'Jesus is Lord', baptism neither necessitates nor eradicates our human-construct labels of 'class', ethnicity, gender (to which we might add, neuropathways, sexuality...) Instead, we are baptised into Christ and His gloriously diverse Body, the Church. With Communion, we are reminded it is 'the Lord's table', not ours; who are we to deny others access? Jesus served Thomas, (knowing Thomas would doubt Him), Peter (knowing Peter would deny Him), and Judas (knowing Judas would betray Him). Whilst we are used to eating with just a few who, coincidentally, like us and are like us, Communion reminds us we belong to a gloriously diverse Church family – the only thing we have in common is Christ! We receive Communion, not because of who *we* are and what *we* have done (or not), but because of *Christ* alone – who He is and what He has done, once *and for all*. In His brokenness, our brokenness finds healing and wholeness. Both baptism and Communion engage our plurality of human senses and learning styles to confer our belonging to, and participation in, Christ's new community, as we eagerly anticipate '*Act Six: Heaven (The End!)*'.

> **To think about...**
> When is *your* church like a glimpse of Heaven? What would make it even more heavenly?

Act 6: Heaven (The End!)

What do you imagine Heaven to be like? The cliché is harp-playing angels with fabulous wings perched on fluffy clouds. To be honest, some depictions make eternity sound hard work. Even the best worship services can wain if they go on too long! Mercifully, Heaven is not so much the *quantity* of eternal life, rather the *quality* of that life – so perfectly Shalom it never ends. Unlike Earth, Heaven is beyond time, space, and matter. It is not just God's heavenly domain, it *is* God; the epicentre of Love.

By '*Act Six: Heaven (The End!)*' the trajectory that Jesus began in '*Act One: Creation*' will be completed as Christ 'makes all things new' (not all new things); finally, life on Earth as God always fully and perfectly intended. So perfect it's as if it's a 'new heaven and new earth'; not re-set to Creation 1.0, as 'very good' as that was, but an entirely *New* Creation.

Though now we see only in part, in Heaven we will see the full and complete picture [1Co.13:9-10]. No wonder Jesus encouraged us to ask, seek, and knock [Mt.7:7-12] and Paul told us to 'work out this salvation' [Php.2:12-13]. There's a humility in accepting that none of us have all the pieces of the heavenly jigsaw. Problems arise when we present our half-truths as the Truth. Only Jesus is *the* Truth [Jn.14:6]. Collectively, *we* (not singular) are God's masterpiece [Eph.2:10]. The 'full picture' only becomes apparent with the diversity of all God's 'image bearers'. Those who exclude some pieces lose sight of God's glorious all-nations Kingdom.

With irresistible grace, 'a great multitude too numerous to count, from *every* nation, *every* culture, *every* people, and *every* language[109]' [Rev.7:9ff] – every human-construct identity or label – will worship the Lamb who was slain. Heaven is not just for 'people like us'. Expect constant surprises! If God desires *all* be saved [1Ti.2:3-4], and Scripture declares that *"at the name of Jesus every knee, whether in heaven or earth, should bow, and every tongue acknowledge Jesus is Lord"* [Php.2:9-11], this must surely include those who are gay as well as straight. It would be odd if what God desires and promises isn't possible for one segmented 'nation'/ culture/ people, yet is possible for everyone else. With the Bible, all always means ALL[110].

Whilst on earth God helps to meet our needs (physical, mental, social, emotional, and spiritual) by giving us those we dwell amongst (which is why we are the losers if we despise those who are God's gift to us); in Heaven it is God who dwells with us, meeting all our needs most perfectly [Rev.21:3]. In Eden it was possible for humanity to hide from God [Ge.3: 8-9], but in Heaven the intensity of God's Presence, His Glory, will render that impossible. That leaves no scope or desire for sin: for example, no discrimination, exploitation, greed, homophobia, racism, or violence (be that physical, psychological, emotional, religious). The 'water of life' river that flows from the throne of God, connecting 'Act One: Creation' [Ge.2], 'Act Three: Israel' [Ez.47], and 'Act Four: Jesus' [Jn.4] to the New Jerusalem [Rev.22], sustains the 'tree of life' with its leaves for the healing of the *nations*. (Remember, 'nations' is shorthand for all our human-construct labels, including myriad LGBTQ+ identities and communities.) Whatever suffering, pain, sickness, trauma has been experienced in the past will be healed, with no possibility of recurrence. There will be no more tears, death, mourning, crying, or pain – ever. [Rev.21:4]. For those who have experienced so much pain, who've cried and mourned the loss of those that lost their lives to injustice and intolerance, Heaven is Sanctuary. The New Jerusalem is a celebration of all that God is and all that God has created; no longer just promises of, or even miraculous 'heaven on earth' moments; simply and completely Heaven – for all eternity.

As we've seen, the Christ-as-Groom/ Church-as-Bride metaphor describes the mutual love and intimacy God and humanity will enjoy together for all eternity. If we still needed proof that this is metaphor, in Heaven we, the 'Bride', are to marry the *'Lamb'* [Rev.19:6-9]. If this too is applied literally then it would suggest the unconscionable: humans are to have intimate sexual relationships with animals. Literally, no one is suggesting that!

On earth, our relationships, when healthy, can give us a heavenly taste of what is to come as we anticipate being united intimately with Christ. It's why it's so cruel to deny those who are LGBTQ+ even the possibility of this foretaste. In Heaven, even our friendships and 'till death us do part' relationships are surpassed by the perfection of relationship with Risen Christ. As Jesus said, *"At the Resurrection people will neither marry nor be given in marriage"* [Mt.22:30]. This being so, it's curious why some invest so much energy trying to ensure sex and marriage remains only heterosexual when the very notion of human relationships and marriage is only temporary – not a feature of Heaven, God's domain.

> **To think about...**
>   1. What do you find helpful about this, my metanarrative?
>
>   2. What, if anything, would you add, amend, or omit from it?
>
>   3. Write your own better metanarrative of the Bible.

23

To inclusion AND BEYOND!

The 40,000 churches in the UK[111] represent a wide range of attitudes towards LGBTQ+ inclusion. Some who are queer hold that same-sex attraction is wrong (sinful) because they believe (or have been led to believe) it is a deviation from God's intended heterosexual order. Their response has been to seek forgiveness (for their sinful *thoughts/ desires*) and healing (so they won't succumb to sin). They pray "God, make me *straight*". Tragically, elements of the Church have compounded the inner turmoil felt by many gay Christians by the application of abusive 'conversion therapies'. Yet, thoughts are not in themselves sinful. Wasn't Jesus tempted in *every way* and yet did not sin [Heb.4:15]? Might it be more sinful to deny what God has declared good?

Others hold that, whilst same-sex *attraction* is not sinful, having a same-sex *relationship* is. They too have sought forgiveness (this time, for their sinful *actions*). They accept their sexual orientation but more as a curse or cross they must bear. They pray "God, make me *celibate*". But in doing so, if God declared it was not good for a person to be alone, celibacy is both a life-style choice and a calling (it's not just that someone doesn't have someone to have sex with). It can apply to all, irrespective of sexual orientation.

Another response comes from those who accept their sexual orientation and live without restraint. They pray, "God, make me _exempt_". But, it's not that 'straight' Christians must live according to God's Way whilst queer Christians can do whatever they please.

Far more positive are those who accept their sexual orientation as just another facet of their unique 'made in the image of God' character. They pray, "God, make me _faithful_". This is what I believe a healthy response to same-sex attraction should be.

Rejecting churches

Some churches and Christians are very clear: their reading of the Scriptures leaves no room for LGBTQ+ inclusion and equality. Whilst I do not agree with them, I respect their transparency and right to hold such a view. Those who are gay, and their allies, know to stay away. No one wants to be preached against simply for existing.

Silent churches

Many churches are simply silent on sexuality (as they are on ethnicity, gender, and many other contemporary issues.) Either uncomfortable with the discussion or fearful of the consequences, they seek uniformity in their collective silence. Whilst some individuals, including their ministers, might be secretly supportive of LGBTQ+ inclusion _as a theory_, they may be too afraid or ambitious to 'speak out'. Those at the more tolerant end adopt an unspoken contract: we'll 'turn a blind eye' if you act 'straight'. 'Don't ask/ don't tell' might feel expedient but it's far from honest, requiring gay people to keep their 'secret', thus reinforcing feelings of shame and judgement.

Welcoming churches

Luke Dowding, Chief Executive of OneBodyOneFaith and Chair of *Affirm: Baptists Together for LGBTQ+ Inclusion*, sees a vital distinction between churches that are welcoming, inclusive, or affirming[112]. He says, "Many churches would attest to providing a welcoming space for all, particularly during their times of corporate gathered worship. A 'theology of welcome' is demonstrated in an open-door policy for everyone." It all *sounds* very welcoming and accepting. However, it soon becomes apparent that 'all' means 'some'. Whilst those who are same-sex attracted are welcome to *attend*, restrictions are placed on their baptism, membership, communion, visible ministry, or leadership. They are welcome to *attend* worship but not *serve* on the worship team; to *receive* teaching but not *deliver* it. The profiling of heterosexual couples ('this is Steve, with his wife Emma'), alongside the invisibility of those who are LGBTQ+, is another clue. The church is a WINO – Welcome In Name Only. Though welcoming churches appear attractive, like a Venus flytrap (Dionaea Muscipula), they are anything but safe for unsuspecting LGBTQ+ visitors. They want your attendance and are nice to your face but, privately or in huddles, are judgemental about who you are. Their theology is more akin to rejecting churches; they just don't want you to realise it (until it's too late.)

Some use diversity (or their limited version of it) as a conscience appeaser or promotional tool, celebrating some (but not all) differences of age, ethnicity, gender, physical ability, socio-economic wealth... What's missing from their wordy statements and visible life is, of course, any reference to sexuality.

John Hayward, a declared 'conservative/ traditionalist', uses a blend of data to assert, "All of the denominations in the UK that are currently growing are those whose confidence in the authority of Scripture enables them to stand against progressive ideology"[113]. What's more, he claims, "To date, no growing church [denomination] has adopted same-sex marriage." Conversely, he observes the United Reformed Church, Welsh Independents, Scottish Episcopal Church, and Methodists – all of which permit same-sex marriage – are in decline. From this he concludes growing churches reject same-sex marriage, declining churches succumb to it. I think he's fallen for 'confirmation bias'. Hayward does at least concede, "their position on marriage has not caused their decline! All have been declining since 1960." After all, Brethren, Catholics, and the Salvation Army oppose same-sex marriage and yet are also declining. It's more likely these 'welcoming churches' are growing *despite*, not because of, their rejecting stance. It can take a while for attenders to recognise that, in these churches, 'all' only means 'some', and then they are offered few if any opportunities to explore alternative perspectives. Some stay (the worship is too good); some leave (for more inclusive churches), others leave the faith altogether.

Interestingly, many of these 'welcoming churches' are known for their vibrant worship, charismatic ministry, fervent faith, application-orientated preaching, social action projects, and strong social networks. Whilst I love these aspects about them (it's almost certainly why they are bucking the attendance trend), I long for them to open up to all. Now, there is a growing number of 'ACE'[114] churches: Affirming of LGBTQ+ siblings in Christ; Charismatic in worship; Evangelical in faith and mission. It seems you can have 'Hillsong but affirming'[115]. After all, why should 'conservatives/ traditionalists' have all the good worship?[116] Good examples are Riverside Church [117]in Whitstable, Kent (until recently, part of the Vineyard movement), and St Mary's, Bryanston Square[118]in central London (revitalised by St Paul's Onslow Square and the Holy Trinity, Brompton network).

Inclusive churches[119]

Increasing numbers of churches are moving towards a more inclusive theology, born out of praxis. For some, this 'slippery slope' began with a gradual inclusion of women (gender), and then people of colour (ethnicity), and now, recognising patterns in principles and theology, those identifying as LGBTQ+ (sexuality).

Whilst there are undeniably a few independent churches, like the infamous Westboro Baptist Church in the USA[120] that use 'hate preach' to reject all but white supremacy, others are simply silent on racism. The people of colour who do attend are expected to 'blend in', not challenging racist attitudes, decisions, or authority. When the white majority – the 'norm' who are in control – say, "we don't see colour", they are denying not just skin pigmentation, but also the validity of culture, history, identity, belonging, experience in the workplace, treatment by the police... In other words, all that it means to be black, brown, Asian, South American... Some welcoming churches are pleased that people of colour attend, so long as they 'dial down' their ethnicity and don't expect to be given authority within the church. We, rightly, don't accept this oppression for women or people of colour, neither should we for lesbian, gay, bi, trans, or queer people. Consequently, inclusive churches have begun to do the work required in understanding the impact exclusion has on LGBTQ+ people, as well as proactively attempting to minimise this and mitigate harm.

Luke Dowding warns,

> *"It is often the case that a Minister and a few others may have journeyed towards the point of an 'inclusive theology' before the rest of their community, and so it is entirely plausible for a church to be welcoming but not entirely inclusive – with some who would profess inclusivity. It is important to remember that inclusion requires work, and that if the minister or leadership are inclusive but some in the wider community are not inclusive; or are perhaps fearful of, or hostile to, LGBTQ+ people, then the church is not a safe space for LGBTQ+ people."*

In open spaces that proactively encourage visitors (such as churches), it's never possible to guarantee every encounter is safe; who knows how that after-service chat will go for every person? An inclusive church not only addresses concerns directly with those that cause hurt, making clear what the church collectively believes and why, but it also creates a culture that lives and breathes inclusion – because of, not despite, the Bible.

A genuinely inclusive church proactively identifies, and then systematically removes, barriers that prevent people from participating, belonging, thriving. At its heart is the genuine belief that life feels better when we are all included. Consequently, it places no direct *or indirect* restrictions on LGBTQ+ people's participation, for example, in baptism, membership, communion, visible ministry, or leadership roles. It is 'access all areas'.

Being inclusive can sound and feel great – if you are privileged heterosexual. Then it's about benevolently bestowing power on others, which, of course, is another way of reinforcing one's own greater power. In this spectrum, inclusive churches still retain an asterisk, with a "yes, but.." small print. Yes, you are included; but no, we still won't marry you. Illogically, they say to straight couples, "Don't just 'live together', commit yourselves in covenant marriage", but tell gay couples, "We can't (or still won't) marry *you*, so 'live together'."

Whilst recognising what many inclusive churches have been through to get to this point – including how long it's taken, and how painful at times it's been – it's nothing in comparison to the pain LGBTQ+ communities have experienced at their exclusion from Christ's Body, the Church. Those who are gay need more than inclusion; they need nothing less than total affirmation of what it means for them to be made in God's image. No asterisk. No small print. It's to inclusion *and beyond*.

Affirming churches

What is the 'and beyond' of inclusion? It is when *all* people made in the image of God – whatever their ethnicity, gender, neuropathway, or sexuality – can be truly and freely the person God has uniquely and wonderfully made them to be. No small print. No asterisk.

Going 'and beyond' for LGBTQ+ people means the one remaining exclusion is finally removed as the church affirms same-sex couples' equal right to marry, publicly committing themselves to each other and God and as they make their sacred vows to one another. Affirming churches are pro-marriage, in a way that those that restrict marriage only to heterosexual couples are less so. *"What God has joined together, let no one separate"* [Mt.19:6].

Whilst an inclusive church might be working towards registering their building for the solemnisation of same-sex marriages, an affirming church already has. There is no more debate; it is finally a 'settled matter'. This demonstrates the church's collective and unequivocal commitment to being a 'safe space', a place of Shalom, for those who are lesbian, gay, bi, trans, or queer. Yes, there will always be a few individuals with different attitudes (there's no 'thought police' and every 'newcomer' has to start the affirming journey again), nevertheless, the settled view of this church is positively affirming of those who are LGBTQ+. No-one can ever guarantee all interactions between attenders will be positive, and that no one will ever be left feeling uncomfortable or hurt. But at least there's a commitment to addressing and educating as it arises, using the model given by Jesus [Mt.18:15-19].

The step from 'inclusive' to 'affirming' is small, especially in comparison to that from 'welcoming' to 'inclusive', but it is crucial. Running a marathon is daunting: so much hard work, pain, determination. Yet, there is also immense satisfaction in discovering what your body was always capable of; you will have achieved something that many others won't. So, imagine, having run 26 miles, you stop just 385 yards short of the finishing line. A marathon is 26.2 miles. Those final yards are vital. For most of us, our aim is not to come first or be the fastest; it's to complete the course. Anyone can start a marathon, far fewer cross the finishing line. If you have put all the effort in to becoming genuinely inclusive, don't 'pull up short';

complete that final stretch and become officially 'affirming'. Remember, it's to inclusion *and beyond*.

> *"Therefore, since we are surrounded by such a great cloud of witnesses, let us throw off everything that hinders and the sin that so easily entangles. And let us run with perseverance the race marked out for us, fixing our eyes on Jesus, the pioneer and perfecter of faith."* Hebrews 12:1-2

Registering for same-sex marriage puts an end to *"Yes, but.."*. It signals to those who are lesbian, gay, bi, trans, or queer that this particular church is serious about inclusion, providing 'access all areas'.

The aim is not just to liberate same-sex couples from the denial of marriage, but also heterosexual couples from the shackles of patriarchy which renders one the property of the other. In the UK today, many 'traditional weddings' (modelled on the Victorian-era 'white wedding' trend[121]) still involve one man, the Father of the Bride, giving away his daughter to be married to another man, the Groom. Same-sex weddings demand a fresh look at language and liturgy, and the assumptions behind them. Everyone wins when everyone is included.

What do we mean by 'marriage'? Surely, it's more than just a couple's 'Big Day' or a certificate? Some couples are officially 'married' but it's in 'ring and certificate only'; they're not living the 'one flesh' life – be that physically, emotionally. Others aren't officially 'married', and yet live faithfully as a couple, even securing property and raising children together. In the eyes of God, who's more married? We should not confuse a wedding with a marriage. That said, there is something beautiful, romantic, and humbling about a couple publicly declaring their "till death us do part" love for each other, in the presence of God and those who know them best.

Securing a licence for same-sex marriages is a moment for celebration. For most churches, it marks the end of a long process. Moses was a high-impact leader. Yet he discovered that leading people out of oppressive slavery in Egypt, even courageously crossing the Red Sea, was far easier than entering the Promised Land. Despite his obvious leadership qualities, a journey of just 250 miles took forty years to complete; all because of resistance, bitterness, and in-fighting within the community. In the end, despite it being his dream and getting within sight of it, it fell to Joshua, not Moses, to finally cross the River Jordan into that land 'flowing with milk and honey'. It's a reminder for leaders to persist with courage and grace for the long-haul.

And yet, affirming is not a policy or a licence, it is an attitude of the heart and mind, and as such requires a lifelong commitment. It's never finished; there is always so much more to understand, do, and become; new people to educate. Crossing the River Jordan was a profound moment; the challenge then was to live in the new freedom.

To think about...

1. To what extent is your community engagement and mission helped or hindered by your church's current attitude towards those who queer?

2. Which heading best describes your church as it currently is: Rejecting, Silent, Welcoming, Inclusive, Affirming? Why?

3. Which type of church do you aspire to be? Why? What, if any, next steps do you need to take?

Repentance

Have you noticed, when they mess up, politicians and institutions often speak of their 'regret'. They rarely say 'sorry'. Instead, they deflect, "If *you* have taken offence at my actions or words, it is a matter of some *regret*." Advised by lawyers and accountants, they'll stop short of accepting responsibility or liability. Yet, wordy statements of regret are no apology. To inclusion *and beyond* goes further. Jesus began with a very simple and direct message: *"Repent. For the Kingdom of Heaven is near"* [Mt.4:17]. Repentance involves actively listening to those hurting, confessing the pain we have caused, giving and receiving grace, making restitution, and changing our ways.

Few can deny the wrongs done by the Church to LGBTQ+ individuals and communities. It is profoundly hurtful to know that you are judged by others to be sinful simply by virtue of your existence, in a way that heterosexual people are not. Just a few examples of appalling treatment are:

* Whispering and ostracising – bullying;

* Withholding Communion, believers' baptism/ Confirmation, or church membership;

* Refusal to dedicate/ christen a same-sex couple's baby (as if the baby is at fault);

* Denying the possibility of marriage, then blaming gay couples for not being married;

* Abusive 'conversion therapy' or 'coercive celibacy';

* Misuse of safeguarding policies to censure or expel LGBTQ+ people, whilst failing to protect them from mistreatment;

* Removal of a youth leader, small group leader, worship leader simply for being gay;

* Refusal to appoint, or the decision to dismiss, a church minister simply because of their same-sex attraction/ sexuality or relationship;

* Failure even at a funeral to acknowledge the deceased's committed same-sex partner;

* Silence of the majority and their failure to speak out.

Whilst it's good to celebrate progress, deeper engagement with LGBTQ+ inclusion must surely lead to times of genuine repentance for past attitudes, beliefs, and actions – the sins of omission and commission. The Church Collective has not loved those who are same-sex attracted in the way that God does. And we've used God's name to back up our own prejudices. To hurt others, is to hurt God whose image they bear. Jesus made clear, *"Whatever you did for one of the least of these brothers and sisters of mine, you did for me"* [Mt.25:40].

The Greek word for repent, 'metanoia', means to 'change direction', 'change your thinking or attitude'. True repentance is demonstrated by action, not just words. Jesus said, *"If you are offering your gift at the altar and there remember that your brother or sister has something against you, leave your gift there in front of the altar. First go and be reconciled to them; then come and offer your gift"* [Mt.5:23-24]. It's clear, repentance is not just for 'others' to demonstrate, it's for you and I also.

Be sensitive not to inflict further pain on those you are seeking forgiveness from. Be aware just how tired or weary they may be of clumsy religious gestures. Well-intended but thoughtless overtures can trigger further emotional distress as feelings or memories associated with past traumatic experiences are brought back to the fore. We should not underestimate the level of trauma many gay siblings-in-Christ have endured.

Sometimes, we have to repent, not just for what *we* have said or done, but also for the 'sins of our fathers'. Oppressive attitudes today have roots that go back into previous generations. Those that commit 'hate crimes' today against LGBTQ+ communities are expressing what the Church historically told everyone to believe. The collective Church carries some responsibility for every incident today of 'gay bashing', physically or verbally. That should 'break us'. Forgive *us our* sin, as we forgive those that sin against us.

We rightly repent over the historic injustices women and people of colour have experienced, and specifically for the horrors of the Atlantic slave trade; not just because it was so unimaginably evil at the time (which of course it was), but because of its compound 'white privilege'. I recently played a small part in the planning of an act of repentance and reconciliation involving white and black Christians/ churches, held in a UK football stadium. It was a necessary, powerful and, I believe, hopeful step in 'calling out' racism. Anti-racist work, helped by profound black theology, is becoming more mainstream. My hunch is that we'll be back in years to come, this time for an act of repentance and reconciliation with our LGBTQ+ siblings. There was awkward silence in the room when I said this at the final planning meeting.

Lord God, we have sinned against you; we have done evil in your sight.

Most merciful God, Father of our Lord Jesus Christ,

we confess that we have sinned in thought, word and deed.

We have not loved you with our whole heart.

We have not loved our LGBTQ+ neighbours as ourselves.

In your mercy forgive what we have been, help us to amend what we are,

and direct what we shall be; that we may do justly, love mercy,

and walk humbly with you, our God. Amen.

To think about...

1. What, if anything, is the Holy Spirit nudging *you* to repent of? What do you need to do?

2. How does the Church repent for historic sins?

24

Conclusion

The 'red thread' of Christ's saving work which runs through the six acts of the Bible from Genesis to Revelation is the means by which all may be saved [Ac.4:12]. This Gospel is so much more than just reciting the 'four spiritual laws', that transactional formula promoted in the 1950s age of 'mass evangelism'.[122] With Jesus, it wasn't so much, 'How do I and my friends get to Heaven?'; it was far more about, 'How do *we* bring Heaven to Earth for all?' If Heaven is God's domain – the epicentre of all that God values, does, and is, undiluted by flawed (sinful) us – then salvation is so much more than securing my place in Heaven. With 'righteousness, peace, and joy' [Ro.14:17] it also brings an end to abuse, consumerism, exploitation, greed, homophobia, judgmentalism, oppression, racism, sexism – and all other 'bad news' evils that deny the image of God in those that God has made and loves.

In the New Testament, 'gospel' appears 93 times and means 'good news'; its Greek form εὐαγγέλιον / 'euaggelion' is what gives us the English words 'evangelist' and 'Evangelical'. Evangelicalism is at its most authentic when it strives to bring and be good news to all, with a bias to the least, lost and last. Just two hundred years ago, the Church was deeply divided over the issue of slavery. 'Traditionalists' argued from both the Bible and their own moral frameworks that slavery was justified – a reflection of God's order within humanity. Evangelicals like William Wilberforce (1759-1833), along with radical Quakers, helped move the discourse from 'sin as slavery' to 'slavery as sin' by relentlessly demonstrating that those being so oppressed were made in God's image. It eventually led to the Slavery Abolition Act 1833 and the gradual ending of slavery that we so take for granted today. To strive for the liberation of lesbian, gay, bi, trans, and queer people – Divine 'image bearers' – should also be an instinctive response for all Evangelicals.

Those who oppose LGBTQ+ inclusion argue, quite rightly, that nowhere does the Bible give an unambiguous and positive endorsement of same-sex relationships and equal marriage. It doesn't; but then, no one is claiming that it does. To this, it must also be conceded, tongue-in-cheek, neither does the Bible give a clear endorsement of electricians, helicopters, a gluten-free diet, or most medical treatments. Does taking the Bible seriously mean we only ever do what it *specifically* endorses – and reject everything that it doesn't? If same-sex relationships and equal marriage are to be precluded because they are not specifically commended in the Bible, to be consistent, we would also need to rule out everything else the Bible doesn't mention. That's my coffee gone! Life would be very limited, with constant checking of the 'rule book'. This would begin to sound more like law than grace; what is known as Biblicism (never used as a compliment!)

To take the Bible seriously is to live freely within its boundaries. Genesis paints a picture of *freedom*, but with some *conditions* for our well-being: we are free to do anything unless God tells us otherwise. Hence, God told Adam (humanity), "*you are free to eat from any tree in the Garden; but you must not eat from the tree of the knowledge of good and evil*" [Ge.2:16-17]. Just because hair straighteners are not mentioned in the Bible, doesn't mean it's wrong to straighten your hair. Life as we know it today would stop if we ruled out anything and everything not specifically endorsed in the Bible. Instead, we are called to live freely, obediently, and with wisdom. God has set Creation's default setting to 'permissive', not 'prohibitive.'

Today we are talking about lesbian, gay, bi, trans, or queer _relationships_: ones which are consenting, faithful, monogamous, life-bringing. What the Bible warns against, as we have seen, is _abuse:_ male rape, child abuse, sex-trafficking, slave master abuse of power towards their slaves. The Bible's warnings against _abuse_ are vital but must not be confused with the same-sex _relationships_ we are talking about today. Just because the Bible rightly condemns rape, child abuse, sex-trafficking/ Temple prostitution, and slave owning and slave masters' abuse of power towards their slaves, doesn't mean God also condemns the consenting, faithful, monogamous, life-bringing same-sex relationships that we recognise today. They are not a like-for-like comparison.

If, as some claim, God opposes same-sex relationships and equal marriage, nowhere in the Bible does it say _why_. What is so bad about being gay? Of course, it could be said that the Bible doesn't explain why stealing is also wrong, and yet, it's easy for people – of all faiths and none – to understand why theft is morally wrong. It's much harder for people, both in and beyond the Church, to accept why God would oppose LGBTQ+ inclusion. Most can rationalise why stealing, drunkenness, slander, and swindling (the sins of 1 Corinthians 6) are wrong. But what's the harm in being lesbian, gay, bi, trans or queer? To respond, 'because God is holy' risks transferring on to God our own imperfect and biased understandings of what we believe are right and wrong – precisely what the Third Commandment warns against.

Despite vociferous opposition from some ardent 'conservatives/ traditionalists', like the _Global Anglican Future Conference (GAFCON)_[123]and _Evangelical Baptists_[124], it feels like momentum is building for inclusion _and beyond_. I think we're finally reaching a 'tipping point'.

A recent survey of Anglican clergy by _The Times_ and _The Sunday Times_[125] found that 53.4% now want permission to marry gay couples in church, with just 36.5% against. This represents a reversal in just a decade; in 2014, 39% were in favour, and 51% against. What's more, 64.5% of priests in England now back an end to the teaching that "homosexual practice is incompatible with Scripture." Only 29.7% said this teaching should not change. The Survey found that 63.3% of Anglican priests believe that gay clergy should be allowed to enter into civil partnerships or equal marriage with their partners[126], with just 28.7% opposing it.

This is at odds with the official position of both the Church of England and worldwide Anglican Communion. The 2022 Lambeth Conference, faced with well-publicised disagreement and a plurality of views (and boycotted by bishops from Nigeria, Rwanda, and Uganda), 'affirmed the validity' of its previous 1998 *Resolution 1.10:* "homosexual practice is incompatible with the Scriptures" and "marriage is between a man and a woman." Whilst it averted schism, it nevertheless felt to many a missed opportunity.

And yet, just six months later, the Church of England's General Synod agreed to same-sex couples receiving a blessing in church after a civil marriage or civil partnership, enabling them to 'give thanks, dedicate their relationship to God, and receive God's blessing'. Whilst this, for me, is a small step in the right direction, it's an illogical position; in effect saying, God blesses what the Church still prohibits.

In addition to the theological case, the Rt Rev Stephen Croft, Bishop of Oxford, makes the point that uniquely as the state church, Anglican parishes have a duty to serve the whole of the community, not just their adherents.[127] Everyone who lives in a parish has, historically, had the right to be married and to be baptised in the parish church.

Whilst most 'top down' denominations must agree one uniform approach for all their member churches to follow, Baptists (my own tradition) are 'bottom up' 'congregational' in governance. Each Baptist congregation has freedom to determine and is responsible for its own path, ethos, theology, finances, appointments... This is enshrined in the historic Baptist Declaration of Principle, which states:

> 1. That our Lord and Saviour Jesus Christ, God manifest in the flesh, is the sole and absolute authority in all matters pertaining to faith and practice, as revealed in the Holy Scriptures, *and that*

each church has liberty, under the guidance of the Holy Spirit, to interpret and administer His laws.

2. That Christian Baptism is the immersion in water into the Name of the Father, the Son, and the Holy Spirit, of those who have professed repentance towards God and faith in our Lord Jesus Christ who 'died for our sins according to the Scriptures; was buried, and rose again the third day.'

3. That it is the duty of every disciple to bear personal witness to the Gospel of Jesus Christ, and to take part in the evangelisation of the world.

Consequently, Baptists Together (the national Baptist Union of Great Britain) does not give a view on the rights or wrongs of equal/same-sex marriage. Though most Baptist churches maintain a 'traditional' definition of marriage as being only between a man and a woman, others are 'affirming' of same-sex couples, with a small (but growing) number registered or registering for equal marriage. This local liberty could have made decisions so much easier for Baptists – simply let each local church decide for itself. What unites Baptists, is not the uniformity derived from all 1,800+ Baptist churches being and believing the same (because we don't!); our unity is found in us all being 'in Christ' – Jesus, the Head of the Church, is our unity. Whatever our differences, we are family – Baptists Together! This has sufficed for a plethora of differences, including: the ordination of female ministers or male-only leadership; charismatic gifts or the cessation of gifts; reformed or free-will election; divorce and re-marriage... Until that is, the question of LGBTQ+ inclusion is raised. Then, suddenly, the conservative push has been for a centralised policy privileging the heterosexual status quo. We are witnessing conservative and progressive tectonic plates vying to change the landscape. Despite this, I'm convinced we're edging ever closer to inclusion *and beyond*.

As I make my closing speech, I have sought to articulate how and why I, as an Evangelical Christian, have come to affirm same-sex relationships and equal marriage. I hope you have found aspects of this book enlightening, encouraging, even stretching. If you have, what's changed for you? What should be your next step? For example, how will you be more of an ally to your LGBTQ+ siblings?

Be an ally

Joseph was a Jewish Levite from Cyprus. Without him, the New Testament would have been thirteen books short, John Mark wouldn't have written the Gospel of Mark, Pharisee Saul wouldn't have become Apostle Paul, and followers of *The Way* wouldn't have been called Christians. You and I know him by his nickname, Barnabas, meaning 'son of encouragement'. When the Church was cautious about Paul, unconvinced that he could be a disciple, Barnabas became his ally [Ac.9:26-27]. Later, when 'outsider' Gentiles first started to believe in Christ, and the Church in Jerusalem was again suspicious, it was Barnabas who became their ally [Ac.11:22-26]. He went, saw, listened, encouraged, created safe spaces, celebrated, and remained alongside them for considerable time, enabling others to grow in their faith and ensuring their inclusion. Good allies, like Barnabas with Paul and John the Baptist with Jesus, know their place: *"He/she/they must become greater; I must become less"* [Jn.3:30]. Yet, Barnabas was also willing to speak out, when necessary.

Being a good ally is not a calling for some, it's a duty of all. As Dr Martin Luther King famously wrote from a prison cell:

> **"The ultimate tragedy is not the oppression and cruelty by the bad people but the silence over that by the good people."**

Change will only happen when the silent majority find their voice and stand as allies with LGBTQ+ communities. Ask your queer siblings how you can best be their ally[128].

- Continue to educate yourself. Don't assume you 'get it'. We've all got so much to learn from each other.

- Listen to queer people. If they 'come out' to you, respond to their tone. Don't 'out' anyone to others.

- Be visible. Wear a lanyard or badge that signals your support for LGBTQ+ inclusion.

- Participate in inclusive events.

- Speak up if others make negative assumptions. Challenge homophobic, bi-phobic or transphobic attitudes.

- Be an agent for change: in your congregation, wider church structures, workplace, community...

> **To think about...**
> 1. To what extent have you been an ally to others in your church, workplace, online or physical communities?
>
> 2. What will you do to be an even better ally to LGBTQ+ siblings?

Last word

Whether or not you have been convinced by my 'workings out', I hope you will at least recognise they reflect my understanding of Scripture. I am 'affirming' *because* of the Bible, not despite it. I respect that some read the same Bible and yet come to different conclusions. None of us can claim a monopoly on truth. For the record, I don't believe those who articulate a heterosexual-only Bible narrative are automatically homophobic (though some clearly are.) Whilst it doesn't always make for close bonding, we're still family!

However, some may reach these final pages and say, "Yes, but.. I still just *feel* it's wrong." For them, the 'love the sinner, but hate the sin' is so deeply ingrained in their cultural or religious 'muscle memory' no amount of logic, theology, or rational argument will make any difference. They don't need anyone to tell them LGBTQ+ inclusion is wrong – they feel it in their spirit. For all their talk of the Bible, they are not willing or able to engage with Scripture or theology. Deep down, they just *know*. I think that <u>*does*</u> stem from homophobia. Though it may be disguised in religious language, it's an irrational fear of, and aversion to lesbian, gay, bisexual, trans, or queer people based purely on prejudice. If not attributing responsibility to God, any negative attitude or belief about queer people is, by definition, homophobic. That you have invested time reading this far suggests this is *not* you! If you need a sense-check, ask yourself:

> **If it turns out God *is* affirming of same-sex relationships and equal marriage, would you be genuinely relieved and excited for what that means for queer people and your church? Or would you have any slight hint of dismay or regret?**

My hope and prayer is that we as Church continue with grace and courage to open up for all who are lesbian, gay, bi, trans, or queer. We're finally reaching a tipping point as more and more Christians add their support.

To inclusion *and beyond!*

Finally, do me a cheeky favour!

If you've found this book helpful, and think others might too, please:

Recommend it to those in your church, social networks...

Post it online e.g. Facebook, Instagram, 'X'... Start a conversation!

Review it on Amazon, Hive, Wordery... It all helps.

Buy it for others. Discounts available for bulk purchases.

Request it from your library.

Appendix 1: A to Z of key words

L anguage both matters and continues to evolve. Here's how I understand some key terms. Do you agree?

Affirming
Recognising and positively celebrating who God has made each individual to be, receiving their uniqueness as God's gift to us all.

Ally
Someone who goes out of their way to demonstrate their public support for and solidarity with an individual or group that has experienced oppression. For example, a straight and/or cis person for LGBTQ+, a white person for people of colour, a man for women...

Asexual/ ace
An umbrella term for those with persistent low to no sexual attraction or interest in having sex (asexual) or an intimate emotional relationship (aromantic).

Bisexual/ bi
Someone who is sexually attracted to their own and one other gender (historically, to both men and women).

Cisgender/ cis
Someone whose gender identity is the sex they were assigned at birth.

Deadnaming

Referring to a transgender or non-binary person by a name they used prior to transitioning, such as their birth name; unintentionally, or a deliberate attempt to deny, mock or invalidate their gender identity.

Demisexual

Someone who only experiences sexual attraction or desire after they have established an exclusive emotional connection with someone.

Evangelical

Someone who believes the historic life, death and resurrection of Jesus as revealed in the Bible was, and still is, 'good news' (gospel) in enabling all people to come back into dynamic and personal relationship with God, one another, self, and Creation, and is proactive in enabling others to experience the same.

Fundamentalist

Someone who takes a very literal approach to each verse of the Bible, denying the need for interpretation or cultural/ textual analysis. Though only emerging in Nineteenth Century USA, as a movement it claimed to uphold the five core fundamentals of Christianity: inerrancy of the Bible, the virgin birth, Christ's death as atonement for sin, bodily resurrection of Christ, historical reality of Christ's miracles.

Gay

A man who is romantically and/or sexually orientated to men. Sometimes also an umbrella term for all lesbian and gay people. Some women prefer to identify as gay rather than lesbian, as do some who are non-binary.

Gender

Often expressed in terms of masculinity and femininity, gender is a social construct that is largely culturally determined and, typically assumed from the sex, assigned at birth.

Gender-dysphoria

This exists when someone experiences deep discomfort or distress caused by a mismatch between their sex assigned at birth and their gender identity.

Gender-fluid

Someone whose gender identity is not fixed; it changes over time.

Heterosexual/ straight

Someone who is romantically and/or sexually attracted to someone of the opposite sex.

Homosexual

Now seen more as a medical term, it's less used in conversation today. Historically, it's a man who is romantically and/or sexually orientated to men.

Homophobia

The fear or dislike of someone, based on prejudice or negative attitudes, beliefs or views about lesbian, gay, bi, or queer people. No-one likes to think *they* are homophobic. "I'm not homophobic, I just believe.." is often a give-away!

Intersex

Someone who was born with biological attributes of both 'male' and 'female', such as sexual organs or chromosomes They may identify as male, female, or non-binary.

Lesbian

A woman who is romantically and/or sexually attracted towards women. Some women prefer to identify as gay rather than lesbian.

Liberal

Someone who interprets the Bible through the lenses of philosophy, rationalism, and scientific reasoning. Shaped by Eighteenth-Century European Enlightenment, it views miracles and incidents/ events in the Bible as myths designed to tell the 'bigger story' of God. It emphasises the humanity of Christ over His Divinity, with Jesus rendered a good role model we can learn from.

Non-binary

Someone who does not identify as either 'male' or 'female'.

Orientation/ sexuality

A person's sexual attraction to other people, or lack thereof.

Pansexual/ pan

Somone whose romantic and/or sexual attraction towards others is not limited by sex or gender. They are attracted to the person.

Pronouns

Words that refer to people's gender, such as 'he/him' or 'she/her'. Some prefer more gender-neutral language and use pronouns such as they/them/their and ze/zir.

Queer

Once viewed as a term of abuse, many LGBTQ+ people have reclaimed it as an umbrella term for all those who are not heterosexual and/ or cisgendered. Not all feel comfortable with it, especially older generations.

Queer theology

The study of God as revealed in the Bible in ways that both liberate those who are LGBTQ+ from homophobic/ transphobic interpretations and narratives and reveal aspects of God that heterosexual lenses filter out.

Questioning

The process of exploring your own sexual orientation and/or gender identity. Jesus said it's healthy to ask, seek, knock!

Sex

Biologically determined, based on chromosomes, and typically evidenced by genitalia and reproductive organs, that lead to human categorisation of either male or female. Sex is different to gender.

Transgender/ trans

An umbrella term describing those whose gender is not the same as, or does not sit comfortably with, the sex they were assigned at birth. A transgender man is someone who was assigned female at birth but identifies and lives as a man. This may be shortened to trans man or FTM (female-to-male.) A transgender woman is someone who was assigned male at birth but identifies and lives as a woman. This may be shortened to trans woman or MTF (male-to-female.)

Ze/zir

Gender-neutral pronouns

Appendix 2: Resources

Resources and networks to help you go to inclusion *and beyond!*

Courses and film resources

Creating Sanctuary course

Six film-based sessions (free) to help people in churches listen to and engage with LGBTQ+ voices. How can we make our faith communities/churches a safer place for LGBTQ+ people? See: https://www.creatingsanctuary.org.uk/

How to be a good Christian ally

Three sessions, comprising booklet and video, produced by the Student Christian Movement (SCM) and OneBodyOneFaith. See: https://www.movement.org.uk/GoodChristianAlly

Living in Love and Faith (LLF)

Produced by the Church of England, LLF tackles tough questions and divisions among Christians about what it means to be holy in a society in which understandings and practices of gender, sexuality and marriage continue to change. The LLF Learning Hub (registration required) includes a 5-session film-based course (free). See: https://www.churchofengland.org/resources/living-love-and-faith

Oasis UK Gender Agenda

Watch sessions from the Gender Agenda 2021 Conference. See: https://www.oasisuk.org/gender-agenda-conference-sept-21/

Queer Theology

A podcast, resources and online community. See: https://www.qu eertheology.com/

Refocusing Faithfulness

Six-session course developed by St Mary's, Bryanston Square, exploring the Biblical basis for LGBTQ+ inclusion in the Church – https://www.instagram.com/lets_refocus/

Stop Kicking the Can

A series of short films produced by affirming Baptists. See: https://www.facebook.com/AffirmingBaptistsTogether

The Bible and Homosexuality

Revd Dr Jonathan Tallon, Biblical Studies Tutor at Northen Baptist College, UK, has produced a series of short films. See: https://www.bibleandhomosexuality.org/

Networks

Affirm – Baptists Together for LGBT+ Inclusion. See: https://www.facebook.com/AffirmingBaptistsTogether

Dignity *and* Worth – LGBTQI+ affirming Methodists & Weslyans. See: https://dignityandworth.org.uk/

Diverse Church – creating online safe communities for LGBT+ aged 18-30, 30+ and parents/carers support. See: https://diversechur ch.website/

House of Rainbow – support and encouragement, especially to Lesbian, Gay, Bisexual, Transgender, Intersex, and Queer (LGBTIQ+) people of colour. See: https://www.houseofrainbow.org/

Inclusive Church – a network of churches, groups and individuals that celebrate and affirm every person whatever their ability, age, ethnicity, health, sexuality... See: https://www.inclusive-church.org/

OneBodyOneFaith – originally known as the Lesbian and Gay Christian Movement - and later joined by Changing Attitude England and Accepting Evangelicals – it educates, campaigns for, networks and supports LGBT+ Christians and allies in the UK and internationally. See: https://www.onebodyonefaith.org.uk/

Open Table Network National network of ecumenical LGBTQ+ monthly gatherings across the UK. See: https://opentable.lgbt/

Ozanne Foundation Advocacy, campaigning and education, founded by Jayne Ozanne – https://ozanne.foundation/

Quest – pastoral support to LGBT+ Catholics. See: https://questlgbt i.uk/

Two:23 – network of LGBTQ+ Christians, meeting 5 times a year in London & online https://www.two23.net/

References

1. The Buggery Act 1533 introduced by Henry VIII made homosexuality a criminal office in England, punishable by death. It was repealed and replaced by the Offences against the Person Act 1828. Buggery remained a capital offence until 1861.

2. The Sexual Offences Act 1967 decriminalised homosexual acts in private between two men aged 21 years and above. It applied only to England and Wales. Homosexual acts remained illegal in Scotland until 1980 and in Northern Ireland until 1982. The age of consent for homosexual acts was lowered to 18 years in 1994 and equalised with heterosexual acts by the Sexual Offences (Amendment) Act 2000.

3. Sexual Offences (Amendment Act) 2000.

4. The Employment Equality (Sexual Orientation) Regulations 2003.

5. The Equality Act 2010 covers discrimination at work, equal access to goods and services, education, access to public premises and associations/voluntary groups. It identifies sexual orientation as a 'protected characteristic' group which means people who identify as gay, lesbian, bisexual or heterosexual/straight are protected against:*Direct discrimination*, for example, is refusing someone a job or service because of their sexual orientation.*Indirect discrimination* is making decisions, or a public body planning services, in a way that disadvantages lesbian, gay, bisexual or heterosexual/straight people unless the policy can be objectively justified.*Discrimination by association* is about discrimination of a person because of their association with another person; for example, as a family member or a carer.*Discrimination by perception* is about the discrimination of people based on the perception that they have a particular sexual orientation even if that is not in fact the case.

6. The Civil Partnership Act 2004 gave same-sex couples entering into a Civil Partnership the same rights and responsibilities as married heterosexual couples in the UK.

7. The Marriage (Same Sex Couples) Act 2013

8. https://yougov.co.uk/topics/society/articles-reports/2023/07/03/record-number-britons-support-same-sex-marriage-10

9. See British Social Attitudes Survey 40, National Centre for Social Justice, 2023, p.21-24.

10. See https://yougov.co.uk/society/articles/45868-record-number-britons-support-same-sex-marriage-10

11. See *British Social Attitudes 36 Survey*, National Centre for Social Research, 2019, p.21.

12. Not to mention the hyper-Creationism 'young Earth' claim that our planet is less than 10,000 years old. So the trip to the Natural History Museum is off then?

13. See *Beyond Z: The Real Truth Behind British Youth*, research with 1500 young people conducted (Channel 4, 2022)

14. Some Christians refer to the Bible as being 'infallible' or 'inerrant' as a way of affirming their high belief in, and appreciation for, the Bible but without necessarily knowing what these terms actually mean. *Infallible* means the Bible, every word and sentence, is completely trustworthy and true. It is incapable of being anything other than true. *Inerrant* means the Bible is without a single error. Every word and sentence is exactly and precisely accurate, as God intended. It makes no false, misleading or contradictory statements.

15. For an overview see Alister McGrath's *Inventing the Universe: why we can't stop talking about science, faith and God* (Hodder, 2015)

16. See Pete Ward's *Growing Up Evangelical: youthwork and the making of a subculture* (Wipf and Stock, 2013)

17. I'm quite comfortable with the now-classic 'Bebbington quadrilateral' definition, first outlined in *Evangelicalism in Modern Britain: A History from the 1730s to the 1980s* (Routledge, 1988).

18. Or Conservative Evangelical for that matter.

19. I appreciate this 'short-hand' risks offending many liberal Christians who have a long-held passion for wrestling with the Bible in order to better understand and serve God. To get my point across to others, I ask for their grace.

20. I am evangelical in my love for and commitment to wrestling with the Bible, and in my commitment to enabling others (whether religious or not) to come to know God. I am resolutely *not* 'evangelical' if that means to subscribe to a specific set of conservative 'religious right' dogmas and attitudes towards those of difference (be that of ethnicity, gender, sexual orientation, social status...). Tragically, 'evangelical' has come to mean someone who's anti-women, anti-gay, anti-environment...

21. CH Spurgeon's speech at the Annual Meeting of the British and Foreign Bible Society, May 5th, 1875

22. See examples of how different Bible translations deal with 1 Timothy 1:10-11:

23. So called because many LGBTQ+ people have felt clobbered by the blunt and violent use of these verses.

24. See Gordon Wenham's *Genesis 16-50 Vol 2* (Zondervan, 2015).

25. See Elaine Storkey's *Scars Across Humanity: understanding and overcoming violence against women* (SPCK, 2015)

26. See Rob Bell's most excellent, if bold, *'What Is The Bible: How an Ancient Library of Poems, Letters, and Stories can transform the way you think and feel about everything'* (William Collins, 2017).

27. See Jonathan Tallon's *Affirmative: Why you can say yes to the Bible and yes to people who are LGBTQI+*, (Richardson Jones Press, 2023), p.32.

28. See https://www.gov.uk/government/statistics/hate-crime-england-and-wales-2021-to-2022/hate-crime-england-and-wales-2021-to-2022

29. See https://www.theguardian.com/uk-news/2023/dec/20/brianna-ghey-found-guilty-murder

30. Deadnaming is the act of referring to a transgender or non-binary person by a name they used prior to transitioning, such as their birth name. Deadnaming may be unintentional, or a deliberate attempt to deny, mock or invalidate a person's gender identity.

31. Concubines were taken as wives but without the rights or recognition as wives.

32. Domestic violence doesn't just happen in 'those' (problem) families. It also happens in church families. It happens in church minister's homes too. Checkout http://www.restoredrelationships.org

33. I won't list examples of autistic traits because, as Dr Stephen Shore famously said, "when you've met one person with autism, you've met one person with autism". See https://drstephenshore.com/

34. Dewinter, De Graaf, & Begeer, *Sexual orientation, gender identity, and romantic relationships in adolescents and adults with autism spectrum disorder* (The Journal of Autism Development Disorder, 2017; 47(9):2927-2934). Similarly, Pecora, Mesibov, & Stokes, *Sexuality in High-Functioning Autism: A Systematic Review and Meta-analysis* (The Journal of Autism Development Disorder, 2016; 46(11):3519-3556).

35. See Hille, Simmons, & Sanders (2020). *"Sex" and the ace spectrum: Definitions of sex, behavioral histories, and future interest for individuals who identify as asexual, graysexual, or demisexual.* (2021, The Journal of Sex Research, 57(7), 813–823).

36. Bogaert found it to be 0.4%. See *Demography of asexuality*. In Baumle (Ed.), *International handbook on the demography of sexuality* (2013, Springer: 275–288). Whereas Poston & Baumle measured it as 1%. See *Patterns of asexuality in the United States.* (Sept 2010, Demographic Research, 23, 509–530). However, the England & Wales 2021 Census put it as low as 0.06% (though this only accounts for those who wrote an answer to "other sexual orientation") See Office for National Statistics (ONS), *Sexual orientation, England and Wales: Census 2021* (released 6 January 2023)https://www.ons.gov.uk/peoplepopulationandcommunity/culturalidentity/sexuality/bulletins/sexualorientationenglandandwales/census2021#sexual-orientation

37. See Attanasio, Masedu, Quattrini, et al, https://doi.org/10.1007/s10508-021-02177-4 (Archives of Sexual Behavior/ International Academy of Sex Research, 2022;51(4):2091-2115.)

38. See George & Stokes, *Sexual Orientation in Autism Spectrum Disorder* (International Society for Autism Research, 2018;11(1):133-141.) https://pubmed.ncbi.nlm.nih.gov/29159906/

39. Would Jesus have endorsed the later 'penal substitution' model of the atonement?

40. The first Bible in English to use both chapters and verses was the Geneva Bible published around 1560 AD.

41. See Ben Witherington's Paul's Letter to the Romans: A Socio-Rhetorical Commentary (Eerdmans, 2004) p.73

42. A blended word or portmanteau blends two words to form one new word. We get brunch from blending breakfast and lunch. Paul was a master of this!

43. NT Wright (when writing in more academic mode) or Tom Wright (when writing more popularly) is cited and quoted by conservatives/traditionalists, liberals, and progressives alike to justify their arguments. For example, the Church of England House of Bishops Piling Report Working Group on Human Sexuality (2013) included both 'accepting' and 'rejecting' theological papers – both cited Rt Rev Wright to support their opposing arguments!

44. See Tom Wright's *Paul for Everyone: The Pastoral Letters - 1 & 2 Timothy and Titus* (SPCK, 2013)

45. See Ben Witherington's *The Acts of the Apostles: A Socio-Rhetorical Commentary*, p463 (Eermans, 1998)

46. See Leslie Newbigin's *The Gospel in a Pluralist Society* (SPCK, 1989).

47. I first wrote this in my book *Joined Up: an introduction to youth work and ministry* (Authentic, 2004). This is no new 'fad' of mine.

48. Genesis 19; Leviticus 18:22; Leviticus 20:13; Judges 19; Romans 1:26-28; 1 Corinthians 6:9-11; 1 Timothy 1:10-11

49. See Revelation 7:3-8; 14:1; 14:3-5.

50. Young Earth creationists take the genealogies listed in the Bible as being the complete and literal 'family tree' and trace back from Jesus Christ (Year 0) to Adam (hence their claim that Adam was created less than 8,000 BC, and the earth created just five days before Adam.) Young Earth creationists reject any suggestion that the genealogies were 'snapshots' grouped in patterns to make a point.

51. Genesis 1-3 is poetic in language in the same way that Job poetically describes the earth as having edges, there being storehouses of snow [Job38[.

52. First referred to by Bishop Irenaeus (130-202 AD) in the Second Century and later developed by Augustine of Hippo (354–430 AD), though also featured in some pre-Christian ancient Greek thinking. See J. N. D. Kelly's *Early Christian Doctrines* (Harper Collins, 1978).

53. 'Original Goodness' or 'Original Blessing' was championed by Irish/British early Christian monk, Pelagius (354-360), who rejected Augustine's predestination theology.

54. See John Goldinay's *Genesis for Everyone: Part 1 Chapters 1-16* (SPCK, 2010).

55. In fact, being alone was the very first thing God declared to be NOT good.

56. Complementarianism has been recently championed by the likes of Mark Driscoll, Tim Keller, J I Packer, John Piper, and Terry Virgo.

57. If it helps, using John Calvin's (1509-1564) General and Particular distinction, all humanity shares the General calling to procreate, whereas not all individual humans have the Particular calling to do so.

58. Forced marriage, not 'arranged marriage' which requires consent of the person accepting the 'arranged' partner.

59. See David Instone-Brewer's Three Weddings and a Divorce: God's Covenant with Israel, Judah and the Church (Tyndale Bulletin, 41.7 May 1996, p.20)

60. See John 6:35 (I am the Bread of Life); 8:12 (I am the Light of the World); 10:7 (I am the Door); 10:11 (I am the Good Shepherd); 11:25 (I am the Resurrection and the Life); 14:6 (I am the Way, the Truth and the Life); 15:1 (I am the True Vine).

61. See R.V.G. Tasker's *Matthew* (IVP, 1983).

62. For an explanation of the meaning of 'yoke' see Rob Bell's *Velvet Elvis: repainting the Christian faith* (Collins, 2012)

63. Many evangelical commentators make little or no mention of Jesus' reference to different kinds of 'eunuchs'. For example. Stephen *Dray's Discovering Matthew's Gospel* (Crossway, 1998); R.T.France's The Gospel of Matthew (Eerdmans, 2007); R.V.G.Tasker's *Matthew* (IVP, 1983). Even Tom Wright's *Matthew for Everyone: Part 2* (SPCK, 2002).

64. Was Potiphar, as second in command only to Pharaoh, a eunuch? Could he have been awarded a 'wife' as a veneer of respectability, despite being unable to have a sexual relationship? Does this explain why Potiphar's wife was so desperate for sexual intimacy, even with a stranger like Joseph?

65. Was Daniel a eunuch? He was taken into captivity in an age when victorious armies castrated their spoils of war; he served under the Chief Eunuch [Dan.1:3]; Isaiah had prophesised to Hezekiah "some of your descendants, your own flesh and blood who will be born to you, will be taken away, and they will become eunuchs in the palace of the king of Babylon" [2Ki.20:18]; Daniel never married. But the Bible doesn't say.

66. See Tom Wright's *Paul for Everyone: The Early Christian Letters - James, Peter, John and Judah* (SPCK, 2011)

67. Jonathan Tallon, *Affirmative: Why you can say yes to the Bible and yes to people who are LGBTQI+* (Richardson Jones Press, 2023), p.79-82.

68. The Holy Bible, New International Version (International Bible Society, 1984)

69. See Ben Witherington's *Conflict & Community in Corinth: A Social-Rhetorical Commentary on 1 & 2 Corinthians* (Eerdmans, 1995), p.171.

70. Have you noticed how churches that only permit men to be leaders, try and present themselves as being egalitarian by having each leader photographed with his supportive, but passive, wife.

71. See John Shelby Spong's, *Rescuing the Bible from Fundamentalism: A Bishop Rethinks the Meaning of Scripture* (HarperOne, 2001), p.117. Whilst he doesn't claim Paul was in a gay relationship, he suggests Paul was celibate because he was gay.

72. See Ben Witherington's *The Acts of the Apostles: A Socio-Rhetorical Commentary*, p.295. (Eerdmans, 1998)

73. See Jarel Robinson-Brown's *Black, Gay, British, Christian, Queer: The Church and the famine of grace* (SCM, 2021)

74. Pride (2014) https://www.imdb.com/title/tt3169706/

75. For a full list of countries that criminalise homosexuality see https://database.ilga.org/criminalisation-consensual-same-sex-sexual-acts

76. House of Rainbow CIC provides safe space and emotional and spiritual support for LGBTQIA+ Christians with Black African Caribbean origins. It began in Lagos, Nigeria, and now from its London-base supports a network in 22 countries. See https://www.HouseOfRainbow.org/

77. See Prof Anthony G. Reddie's *Black Theology* (SCM, 2012), p.55

78. See Prof Robert Beckford's, *Jesus is Dread: Black Theology and Black Culture in Britain* (DLT, 1998), p.61-78

79. See Stanton L. Jones' *A Study Guide and Response to Mel White's What The Bible Does – and Does Not Say – About Homosexuality* (2006) p.14 https://www.wheaton.edu/media/migrated-images-amp-files/media/files/centers-and-institutes/cace/booklets/StanJonesResponsetoMelWhite.pdf

80. See NT Wright's, *Simply Good News: Why the Gospel is news and what makes it good?* (SPCK, 2015).

81. The ninth hour, or 3.00 pm, was the time of prayer and sacrifice at the Temple in Jerusalem. It was also the time of Christ's death. Whilst the "insiders" were at the Temple in Jerusalem doing their 'religious duty', this "outsider", not welcome in the Temple, was having a profound encounter with God.

82. See Ben Witherington's *The Acts of the Apostles: A Socio-Rhetorical Commentary*, p.357. (Eerdmans, 1998)

83. In recent times a sharp debate and dispute has arisen at the national Council of the Baptist Union of Great Britain on whether or not Nationally Accredited Baptist Ministers in a same-sex civil partnership/ equal marriage should be subject to 'gross misconduct' and so lose their Ministerial Accreditation. Currently, the Ministerial Recognition (MinRec) Rules state that any Nationally Accredited Baptist Minister in an equal/ same-sex marriage or Civil Partnership, unless celibate, has committed 'gross misconduct' and so is removed from the Register of Nationally Accredited Ministers ('the Accredited List'). Specifically, Appendix 3, Section 4.3 includes:

"Sexual Misconduct which brings the church and ministry into disrepute. NB This specifically includes sexual intercourse and other genital sexual activity outside of marriage (as defined exclusively as between a man and a woman)."The Baptist Council has been asked to amend this rule. Should the bracketed section be retained or removed? Given the diversity and strength of opinions expressed, Baptist Council are consulting churches and Accredited Ministers (closes 30th Nov 2023). The final decision is for Baptist Council (March 2024). At the time of writing, the outcome of this is not known.

84. Is that a pun?

85. See Ben Witherington's *The Acts of the Apostles: A Socio-Rhetorical Commentary*, p.461. (Eerdmans, 1998)

86. Surely, taking the Lord's Name in vain is not just the avoidance of saying 'TGI Friday'. The Fourth Commandment seems much more about not invoking God's Name or authority to support your own agenda, desires, or prejudices.

87. Other Creeds are available.

88. See Erik Thoennes' http://www.amazon.com/Lifes-Biggest-Questions-Things-Matter /dp/1433526719/?tag=bettwowor0e-20 (Crossway, 2011), and Albert Mohler's *A Call for Theological Triage and Christian Maturity*.

89. Methodist Conference 30th June 2021. Marriage & Relationships Resolution 59-8 https://www.methodist.org.uk/media/21969/conf-2021-59-marriage-and-relatio nships-provisional-resolutions-updated.pdf

90. That's Manchester United Football Club fans lost to the cause!

91. 1845.

92. What a cool name for a band!

93. See Anthony Bogaert & Malvina Skorska, *A short review of biological research on the development of sexual orientation*, Journal of Hormones & Behavior (https://www.sciencedirect.com/journal/hormones-and-behavior/vol/119/suppl/C , March 2020, 104659, https://www.sbne.org/)

94. See Chris McManus' *Right Hand, Left Hand: The Origins of Asymmetry in Brains, Bodies, Atoms, and Cultures* (2002, Harvard University Press).

95. Office for National Statistics (ONS), released 6 January 2023, ONS website, statistical bulletin, https://www.ons.gov.uk/peoplepopulationandcommunity/culturalidentity/sexuality/bulletins/sexualorientationenglandandwales/census2021

96. https://www.livingout.org/

97. https://truefreedomtrust.co.uk/

98. Rev Dt Stephen Finamore, *Towards a Biblical Theology of Marriage* (27/09/2023) http://www.evangelicalbaptist.uk/2022/05/05/towards-a-biblical-theology-of-marriage/

99. Limited atonement is the belief popularised by John Calvin (1509-1564) and the reformed tradition that, though sufficient for all, Christ only died for the sins of the elect (those that God had pre-ordained to believe in Him), and therefore, Christ did not die for those outside of God's grace.

100. See NT Wright's *The New Testament and the People of God* (SPCK, 2013), building on his *Scripture and the Authority of God* (SPCK, 2005), p.122.

101. Except those who have claimed woman are biologically not qualified to be Priests because only men can truly represent Christ. Another example of misreading the Scriptures that has taken Centuries to challenge.

102. See https://news.yale.edu/2015/09/02/seeing-forest-and-trees-all-3-trillion-them

103. Shepherds were judged to be 'unclean' because their sheep *trespassed* onto other's people's land, their absence from Temple life due to work patterns 'out on the hills', and their contact with unclean animals and their faeces/ body fluids.

104. "Physician, heal yourself" is nowhere in the Old Testament, yet it had become part of the 'traditionalist' narrative, as if it was. To this we could add, "God helps those who help themselves", "God is in control", "Cleanliness is next to Godliness", and "love the sinner, hate the sin."

105. See NT Wright, *John For Everyone Part 1 Chapters 1-10*, (SPCK, 2002), p.112.

106. See John Stott, *The Message of Ephesians* (IVP, 1979) p.134.

107. NT Wright has written much. See his *Surprised by Hope* (SPCK, 2011) and *Simply Good News* (SPCK, 2015).

108. For example, Paul gives slightly different versions in 1 Corinthians 12:13 and Colossians 3:11.

109. Language is more than just different dialects; it's also about the *way* we speak and the way we *hear* one another.

110. I find it curious why many Conservative Evangelicals take literally verses that appear to exclude 'others', yet don't apply the same to verses that 'include'.

111. In the UK there are still more churches than pubs!

112. https://www.affirm.org.uk/inclusive-or-affirming?fbclid=IwAR0zOClswzA5igjoyR Fzxt-S6vyLrANyPtH9k8OFA-t4KdhTGCQqxzvLmD0

113. See John Hayward's website, Church Growth Modelling https://churchmodel.org.uk /2022/05/20/uk_church_decline_and_progressive_ideology/

114. Not to be confused with the 'ace' some asexuals use as a shorthand for themselves.

115. I'm grateful to Revd Simon Hall for this observation. https://www.chapela.org.uk/p/ why-we-are-an-inclusive-church

116. Read Vick Beeching's powerful and sobering insight into the world of conservative evangelical worship, *Undivided: Coming Out, Becoming Whole, and Living Free From Shame* (William Collins, 2019).

117. See https://www.RiversideUK.org/

118. St Marys, Bryanston Square, in central London is a large evangelical charismatic Anglican church. See https://www.stmaryslondon.com/

119. Inclusive churches still have a 'yes but..' exclusion. Inclusion is the journey, not the destination.

120. Westboro Baptist Church is a small, unaffiliated independent church in Kansas USA , with no connection to the Baptist World Alliance or any of its national members, that has become infamous for its wide-ranging far right 'hate preach'.

121. Queen Victoria wore a white lace dress for her wedding to Prince Albert in 1840. And sparked a trend which continues for many today. It has everything to do with social etiquette and cultural trend, yet almost nothing to do with Christian marriage or weddings featured in the Bible.

122. *The Four Spiritual Laws* booklet was created by Bill Bright, founder of Campus Crusade for Christ (now known as Cru) as a post-war mass evangelism tool to help people 'convert correctly' to Christianity: 1) God loves you and created you to know Him personally; 2) Man [sic] is sinful and separated from God, so we cannot know Him personally or experience His love; 3) Jesus Christ is God's only provision for man's [sic] sin. Through Him alone we can know God personally and experience God's love; 4) We must individually receive Jesus Christ as Savior and Lord; then we can know God personally and experience His love. Though it's helped many find faith, it's not a model found in the Bible. Jesus simply said, "Come, follow me."

123. See https://www.gafcon.org/

124. See http://www.evangelicalbaptist.uk/ Just like the UK-based *Evangelical Alliance,* it operates more like an alliance of *Conservative* Evangelicals, so this would be better named Conservative Evangelical Baptists.

125. *The Times* and *The Sunday Times* survey analysed 1,185 responses sent out to 5,000 randomly chosen serving priests with English addresses in Crockford's Clerical Directory of Anglican clergy.

126. Anglican clergy have been permitted since 2005 to be in civil partnerships, but only on condition that they remain celibate.

127. See Rt Rev Steven Croft's *Together in Love and Pain* (Bishop of Oxford, 2022) p.14

128. SCM/ OneBodyOneFaith have produced a three-session video-based course called *How To Be A Good Christian Ally.*

Printed in Great Britain
by Amazon

39130167R00119